ROB RENFROE

UNFAILING

Standing Strong on God's Promises in the Uncertainties of Life

 Seedbed    ZONDERVAN REFLECTIVE

Seedbed Publishing, published in partnership with Zondervan Reflective

Unfailing
Copyright © 2019 by Rob Renfroe

Requests for information should be addressed to:
Seedbed Publishing *415 Bridge Street, Franklin, Tennessee 37064*
Zondervan, *3900 Sparks Dr. SE, Grand Rapids, Michigan 49546*

ISBN 978-1-628-24591-2 (softcover)

ISBN 978-0-310-10817-7 (ebook)

ISBN 978-0-310-10818-4 (audio download)

Cover design: Nick Perreault
Interior design: PerfecType, Nashville, Tennessee

Printed in the United States of America

19 20 21 22 23 / LSC / 10 9 8 7 6 5 4 3 2 1

With the deepest gratitude, I dedicate this book to my parents,
Bob and Betty Renfroe, whose immeasurable love
has shaped my life and continues to be unfailing.

CONTENTS

ONE

GOD'S PROMISES TO YOU

Imagine that your death is near. And you know it. You call together those you love and those you have led. What would you say to them?

That's where Joshua found himself. In fact, as he shared his heart with those who were dear to him, he said, "Now I am about to go the way of all [flesh]" (Josh. 23:14).

Joshua had lived a long life—110 years (24:29). Before he spoke to the leaders of Israel on his deathbed, I'm sure he thought about all he had experienced. He had suffered as a young man when his people, the Israelites, were enslaved in Egypt, seemingly to languish there forever, hopeless and forgotten. He had witnessed the mighty, gracious hand of God, who had miraculously set him free and delivered his brothers and sisters from bondage. He was with his leader, Moses, wandering in the wilderness for forty years, fed daily by the manna God provided. He had seen God faithfully lead his people with a pillar of cloud by day and with fire by night. He had watched God go before the Israelites into the promised land, fight their battles, defeat their enemies, and give them a home. Think about the arc of Joshua's life. What he had seen. The lessons he had learned.

You know your death is imminent. You think about your life. You want to leave those you love with words that are true and that will sustain them when you are gone. You want to give them a final blessing they can hold on to and that will hold on to them. So, you choose your words carefully, purposefully. You want to get it right. And Joshua did. Look what he told his people just before he died:

> "Now I am about to go the way of all the earth. You know with all your heart and soul that not one of all the good promises the LORD your God gave you has failed. Every promise has been fulfilled; not one has failed." (Josh. 23:14)

His words to the nation of Israel are as true and his counsel as fitting today as they were the day Joshua spoke them. You can trust the promises of God. They are good and they do not fail. Be obedient. Be courageous. When you understand and when you don't. When life is good and when life is hard. When your friends stand with you and when you stand alone. Act in faith and trust his Word. God keeps his promises.

As Joshua felt his life fading away, he must have asked himself, *What final gift do I have to give? What last lesson do I have to teach? What's the most important truth I can convey to those I love?* The answer was clear: the promises of God are unfailing.

Why was this such a critical word for God's people? Why is it a critical word today? Because life in this world is painful, confusing, and full of problems. Jesus taught us this. It's a promise, really. It's not the kind of promise that we underline in our Bibles and commit to memory, of course. But we should. "In this world you will have trouble" (John 16:33), he said.

The Greek word for trouble (*thlipsis*) in this verse means "suffering" or "tribulation." It carries the idea of being afflicted or harassed. Jesus promises us that we will experience this kind of trouble in our lives. True, he came to bring us abundant life (John 10:10), but he did not promise that life would be easy or without pain.

We may suffer because of what others do to us. Too often we create our own pain because of the foolish or wrong decisions we make. Maybe the worst suffering we endure is when those we love are hurting and nothing we do relieves their pain or makes their lives better. However it comes, in this life you will have trouble. That's a promise.

Still, Jesus said you can experience a life that is abundant and full. But how?

I believe the quality of our lives depends on where we look for strength and wisdom and comfort.

When your way is hard and the night is dark, where do you go for strength? When you're confused and in pain, what do you look to for help? When everything is going well, and you feel that you're winning, but a little voice inside says there must be something more, where do you turn? When you become mature enough to admit that most of your problems come not from the people around you but from the pride and the anger and the greed that live within you, where do you seek the power to change? When nothing makes sense, what do you trust to guide you?

Some People Trust in Their Circumstances

When their lives are good, they're good. But when life is hard, they shatter. As long as their finances are in order, their health is robust, their families are happy, and their jobs are going well—as long as there are no problems they can't handle—they're great. But when tough times come, when life is unfair, when their struggles aren't quickly solved, they become depressed and lethargic, or angry and bitter. They'll often pray, "God, why do I have to go through this? It's not fair. Life shouldn't be so hard."

Live that way, looking to your circumstances for your emotional health and your spiritual stability, and you will be little more than an emotional bubble rising and falling on the waves of fate. If that's you, I hope you will memorize a saying that has helped me over the years: "What happens *in* me is more important than what happens *to* me." You cannot control what the world does to you, but you can always control how you respond. That makes all the difference.

Some People Trust Their Feelings

This is a terrible way to live. It's one of the first lessons we try to teach our children: control your feelings; don't be controlled by them. As one of my mentors, Bill Hinson, often said, "We don't live at the mercy of our moods." He's right. If we want to succeed in life and be faithful to Christ, we must rise above our emotions. We must do

4

what's right and hard in spite of our feelings. But many people are controlled by their emotions. They do only what they feel like doing. And when they feel tired and hopeless and confused, they don't do much of anything.

Everyone who has lived valiantly and who has followed Christ faithfully has had to persevere when it felt pointless to do so. Everyone who has ever acted in faith had to overcome his or her fear. Every person who has made the world a better place has had to continue loving and working when they were discouraged and saw no way to change the world around them.

Your emotions will tell you to feel sorry for yourself, admit defeat, and give up. Live controlled by your emotions and you will never experience the abundant life that requires faith and courage and perseverance.

Our feelings are such poor indicators of our reality that we can't trust them to tell us how we're doing in life. There are people who feel that all is well when the truth is just the opposite. They are so spiritually dull that they don't realize how far they are from God or that they are failing at what matters most. Some of these people are in the church. In Matthew 7, Jesus spoke what may be the most frightening words in the entire Bible.

> Not everyone who says to me, "Lord, Lord," will enter the kingdom of heaven, but only the one who does the will of my Father who is in heaven. Many will say to me on that day, "Lord, Lord, did we not prophesy in your name and in your name drive out demons and in your name perform many miracles?" Then I will tell them plainly, "I never knew you. Away from me, you evildoers!" (vv. 21–23)

It's possible to feel close to God when, in reality, we are very far away.

The opposite is also true. You can feel terrible about yourself and your life when, in reality, you're doing just fine. Many people feel worthless, unloved, and condemned, not because that's how God sees them, but because they grew up in a dysfunctional home where they were constantly criticized and attacked. They came to feel that nothing they ever did was enough. They could never be certain of their parents' love. Without knowing it, they have remade God into the image of their never-satisfied, always-critical father or mother, and their emotions never allow them to feel God's smile upon them.

One of the great joys of being human is our ability to feel intensely. But when our feelings are unhealthy (and all of us have some emotional dysfunction), they can be a curse because they lie to us about our true condition.

Our emotions can blind us to the truth and even derail us. The story of the prophet Elijah's victory over the prophets of Baal is revealing. Elijah had finally exposed the false prophets that had led Israel astray, and the people had destroyed them. Elijah had fought and suffered for this moment for decades. It was the highlight of his life. Yet, in the very next chapter, Elijah was so terribly depressed that he prayed, "I have had enough, LORD . . . Take my life" (1 Kings 19:4).

Elijah went from the highest of highs to the lowest of lows in just a matter of days. Yet, nothing of consequence had changed. God was still God. The false prophets were defeated. Israel had not turned back to Baal. Elijah was still victorious. But *something* had changed, and to the point that Elijah wanted to give up and die. What was different?

Only his emotions.

As a young preacher, every Sunday afternoon after church, I would go home depressed. No matter how many people had said something positive as they left the services, I would still go home feeling bad, not only about the sermon, but about myself. *That was awful*, I would think. *God, I hate myself.*

It was utterly bizarre because I actually thought I preached fairly well. The church was growing. People were very complimentary. Yet every week I went home feeling discouraged.

Finally, I came to a realization. After a restless Saturday night, thinking about my sermon; after getting up at 4:00 a.m. to practice one more time; after preaching three services on a Sunday morning; after experiencing the huge adrenaline rush that comes when you speak in front of others, and the inevitable crash that follows; and after expending the immense amount of emotional energy it takes to be "the man for others" for four hours straight, I was spent, and my emotions were completely out of whack when church was over.

So, I got into the habit of going home, getting something to eat, and taking a good nap. When I got up, guess what? I felt better. Much better. My sermon hadn't changed. What people had said hadn't changed. The church hadn't changed. Nothing had changed except that my body chemistry had returned to normal and I felt different.

All that is to say, our feelings are a bad indicator of how we're doing in life. And it's utterly foolish to trust them or build your life around them. Do that and you will be up and down, encouraged and discouraged, unstable and unpredictable, living at the mercy of your moods. We need something that is more certain and steadfast than our emotions to build our lives upon.

Some People Trust in Their Own Wisdom and Abilities

God has given you a good mind, and he expects you to use it. If it hasn't already, one day life will humble you. You will find yourself in a situation you cannot control or even comprehend. The only question is whether you will recognize the depth of your need, humble yourself, admit your inadequacy, and ask for help.

A short prayer titled "Breton Fisherman's Prayer" expresses well where we find ourselves so often. "Dear God, be good to me; the sea is so wide, and my boat is so small." You will discover that your wisdom is so small when you have a child addicted to drugs. All your bright ideas will prove insufficient and leave you feeling helpless. When your wife is diagnosed with cancer; when you have everything you hoped for but you're still depressed; when your child is embittered toward you; when your marriage is falling apart; when you have failed God and you're covered in shame—you will then learn how wide is the sea, how small is your boat, and how desperately you need God to be good to you.

In the moments that matter most, you will discover that you need a wisdom greater than your own.

Behind every truly great mess you'll find someone whose pride told him that he knew exactly what to do and whose ego prevented him from getting on his knees and asking for help. The question is: Will you be that person—so self-assured and so proud that you will attempt to solve the great problems of life by turning to nothing greater than the wisdom within your own head? Are you so afraid of appearing weak that you will refuse to turn to a strength outside of your own frail body?

Proverbs 14:12 seems to suggest that we are in the most danger when we don't know what we don't know. "There is a way that seems right to a man, but in the end it leads to death." So often, what appears right to us is, at best, incapable of creating a truly successful life. At worst, it is a road to disaster.

You are a strong, magnificent creature made in the image of God. But you are also fallen and flawed and so often fooled into giving your strength to purposes and solutions that do not bring life or create wholeness. The right response to the human condition is not pride and independence, but humility and openness to the help that comes from God and others.

If we cannot trust our circumstances, our emotions, or our own wisdom and strength, what can we trust? There's one thing that never changes. There's one thing that brings life. There's one thing that is sufficient in every situation and that can be trusted when nothing makes sense. And that one thing is the promises of God.

You may be as jaded as I am when it comes to promises. It seems that half the products on the supermarket shelves promise they are "new and improved." I don't believe that. Neither do you. How about this promise: "We're sorry to place you on hold; a customer service representative will be with you shortly"? When I hear that, I know I have time to put the phone down, make a sandwich, wash the car, and play a round of golf. Then there's the Oriental rug store in Houston that has had a sign on its marquee for three decades saying, "Going out of business—50% off" (which isn't as bad as the guy in Dallas who actually named his rug store "Going Out of Business"). They've been promising to go out of business for forty years. Still haven't done it.

Some of us have decided not to believe in promises because, in the past, trusting others and their promises made us vulnerable and brought us much pain: "I will love you for better, for worse, until death do us part." "I'm sorry. I promise, I'll never do it again." "I'll never hurt you." "I'll be here, waiting for you, when you come back."

Open your heart to someone who is unfaithful and disloyal and the pain you suffer may be so great that you resolve to protect yourself by never trusting anyone's promises again.

But we want to believe there are promises we can depend on and people who will keep them. A father, a mother, a brother, or a sister. A wife, husband, a friend. We also want to believe that there is a God who keeps his promises. But how can people who are as jaded as we are trust in the promises of a God we can't see or touch?

Two thousand years before the birth of Jesus, God called a man named Abram, later known as Abraham, to serve and follow him. His calling was followed by a promise: "I will surely bless you and make your descendants as numerous as the stars in the sky . . . and through your offspring all nations on earth will be blessed" (Gen. 22:17–18).

Humankind had rebelled against God, and the world had become corrupt and depraved. So God called a man to begin the story of salvation, and he did so with the promise, not only that he would bless Abraham's physical descendants, but that through those descendants he would bring blessing to all the nations on earth. It was a promise that God would do whatever it took to bring salvation to all people.

If you have read the Old Testament, you know that it is the love story of a faithful God and an unfaithful people. No sooner had Yahweh delivered his people from slavery in Egypt then they yearned to go back so they could eat their captors' meat. Not long afterward, they worshipped a golden calf instead of the God who had freed them from bondage.

But God remained faithful. He brought them into the promised land, flowing with milk and honey. What did they do? They turned to idols—again. Still, when they were attacked, God raised up deliverers like Gideon to defeat their enemies. When they were taken into exile by foreign kings, God returned them to their land. All throughout their many years of disobedience, he sent prophets to speak to his people, calling them back to himself.

No matter how gracious and faithful God was to his people, the story was always the same: a loving God, forgotten and rejected by an ungrateful people. The prophet Isaiah mourned their unfaithfulness: "My loved one had a vineyard on a fertile hillside. He dug it up and cleared it of stones and planted it with the choicest vines. He built a watchtower in it and cut out a winepress as well. Then he looked for a crop of good grapes, but it yielded only bad fruit" (Isa. 5:1–2).

In the verses that follow, God himself speaks. "Now you dwellers in Jerusalem and people of Judah, judge between me and my vineyard. What more could have been done for my vineyard than I have done for it? When I looked for good grapes, why did it yield only bad?" (vv. 3–4).

It would have been so easy for God to give up and walk away. He had every reason to say, "I've done all I can do; I've given all I can give; I've loved all that I can love. I'm through with you."

But our God is faithful and his promises are unfailing. So when we were lost in our sins, when we had rejected the God who loved us, when we had rebelled against his mercy and proven ourselves unworthy and ungrateful, the God of the universe took on human flesh and instead of walking away, he stepped into our world to fulfill the promise he had made.

We Christians have the most interesting concept of God. We describe God as the Trinity—one God in three persons. It's a difficult concept, and no one fully comprehends it. But what we know for sure is that the relationship between the first and second persons of the Trinity—the Father and the Son—is at least as deep and caring as the relationship that a loving earthly father has with his child. To keep the promise God had made to Abraham and to all of humankind, God the Son came into our world, knowing that he would be mocked and rejected, scourged, spat upon, and eventually, crucified. And to keep his promise, God the Father knew he would have to allow it to happen to the One he loved.

Years ago, when *The Passion of the Christ* first arrived in theaters, I waited and waited to see it. I must have been asked a hundred times, "Are you going to see *The Passion of the Christ*? . . . Have you seen *The Passion of the Christ*? . . . I know you've seen *The Passion of the Christ* by now—what did you think? . . . You haven't seen it? Well, you're going to see it, aren't you?"

I'd tell people, "I don't want to see it." And they'd respond: "But why? It's about Jesus." Exactly. It's about the One I love, the One I owe my life to. And I knew what was going to happen. The One I love was going to be beaten and mistreated. A crown of thorns would be forced into his head, and spikes would be nailed into his hands and feet. Evil men would stand around his dying body and call him a fool.

It was only a movie. But I didn't want to see it because I knew it would be painful—and devastating—to see what his enemies did to him. And when I finally watched it, it was.

What if it wasn't a movie? What if it was real, and I was the father and it was *my* son who was suffering that way? What if I saw the nails and the blood and I heard despicable men laughing at his pain? All this done to *my* son—my joy, my heart, my beloved—who had done no wrong and who had harmed no one. His friends have run. His disciples have deserted him. Then, in his lowest moment, as he feels the hot breath of death upon his neck, he feels that even I have abandoned him, and he cries out, "My God, my God, why have you forsaken me?" (Matt. 27:46).

Could I have stayed my hand? Could I have listened to his cries and remained silent? Could I have watched him suffer and have refused to save his life? And for what? To honor a two-thousand-year-old promise? To save people who had been unfaithful to me over and over? To deliver a world that was rebellious and deserving of nothing but judgment and hell?

Maybe I could give my own life, maybe. But my son's? I don't know. Honestly, I don't know.

Everyone is faithful until faithfulness becomes costly. It's only when a price must be paid that you know someone's heart.

Tommy was a big, rugged man. He lived in the country with his wife and their daughter. He was a member of a church I served where most of the members were bankers and lawyers and doctors and business owners. Tommy didn't exactly fit in. He was a laborer and a farmer. Once when I went to see him, he told me, "I don't know how old to expect to live to."

"Why's that?" I asked him.

"Well," he said, "I was just up at the family cemetery, cleaning it up. I looked at all the tombstones and for the first time I realized that none of the men in my family have ever died of natural causes." He said it with a little laugh. But he wasn't joking.

Tommy was different, though, from his family. He had accepted Christ, and his life had changed. He was a good husband and a good father. Tommy was a good man and a good friend to me.

Late one evening, the phone rang. Tommy's daughter had been in an accident. Her date had pulled up behind a car that had stopped at a railroad crossing. For some reason he sped around the car in front of them, and the oncoming train couldn't stop before it was too late.

Suzy was placed on life support, and after a terrible, gut-wrenching week, the decision was made to let her go. I had seen the family at the hospital and prayed with them. But I dreaded this last visit. What would I say? How could I help them process what had happened?

We prayed in a private waiting room before they went to see Suzy for the last time. As we opened our eyes, Tommy looked up at me and said, "Rob, there's something I can't figure out."

Here it comes, I thought, the question I dreaded, the "why did it happen?" question that I had no answer to.

"I just can't understand why. Why did God do it? I'm about to go in there and let my daughter die," he said. "It's the hardest thing I've ever had to do. Just thinking about it rips my heart out. I wouldn't do it if there was any other way. And the question I've been wrestling with is: Why? Why did God do it? He let his Son die when he didn't have to—for me. I just can't figure out why he would love me the way he does."[1]

Why *would* the Father let his Son die in pain and in shame?

Because he made a promise. He told Abraham that he would bring blessing into the world through his lineage.

When God gave us his laws, and his laws did not change our hearts; when he gave us the prophets, and the prophets didn't change our hearts; and when he blessed us with material comforts and wealth, and still our hearts were not changed, he sent his Son to die in our place. He came to keep his word and fulfill the promise he had made no matter what the cost.

Love is faithful. Love keeps its promises. Love suffers for others, even those who are undeserving. And God is love.

You can be sure. In this world you will have trouble. Where will you turn for strength and comfort? Your emotions will mislead. Your circumstances will rise and fall. Your wisdom will prove insufficient. Others will fail you. But God will keep every promise he has made to you because he has already fulfilled the one that cost him the life of his Son. "He who did not spare his own Son, but gave him up for us all—how will he not also, along with him, graciously give us all things?" (Rom. 8:32).

Every promise we will examine in the following chapters, you can believe. You can hold on to them and walk in them, knowing they are strong and sure. Why? Because they are the promises of a God who is faithful. And his promises are unfailing.

Holy God, Father of our Lord and Savior Jesus Christ, by your grace I will trust your promises and stand upon your Word. I so often look to my circumstances, give way to my emotions, and trust in my own wisdom. But you alone have the words of life. You alone can see tomorrow. You alone are good and faithful. So, I will trust your promises because your promises are unfailing. In the name of Jesus, amen.

TWO
THE PROMISE OF FORGIVENESS

There's a double meaning to the word *unfailing* in the title of this book. One conveys the idea that God will never fail to keep his promises. We can trust them and base our lives on them because God is faithful to his Word. It's what Joshua meant when, near the end of his life, he reminded the Israelites that not one of God's promises had failed. Paul reiterated the same trustworthiness of God's promises when he wrote to the Corinthians: "For the Son of God, Jesus Christ . . . was not 'Yes' and 'No,' but in him it has always been 'Yes.' For no matter how many promises God has made, they are 'Yes' in Christ" (2 Cor. 1:19–20).

The other idea inherent in the word *unfailing* is that if we walk in God's promises and stand on his Word, *we* will never fail. Hard times may come; we may experience confusion, loss, and pain; and we may feel overwhelmed—but if we stand on the promises of God, we will come out of the storm stronger, better, closer to God, and more like Christ. Jesus said, "Everyone who hears these words of mine and puts them into practice is like a wise man who built his house on the rock. The rain came down, the streams rose, and the winds blew and beat against that house; yet it did not fall, because it had its foundation on the rock" (Matt. 7:24–25).

Stand on the Word of God. Walk in his promises. And you will not fall or fail.

A great promise you can stand upon is, "I will forgive your sins." You can be forgiven. You can start over, even after you've blown it. Why? Because there is no condemnation for those who are in Christ (Rom. 8:1).

In the Old Testament, through the prophet Jeremiah, God announced that he would make a new covenant with his people that would replace the covenant given to them through Moses on Mount Sinai (Jer. 31:33). This is what he did in the life, death, and resurrection of Jesus.

The old covenant was based on the Law. The new covenant would be based on grace. The old covenant was written on stone tablets. The new covenant would be written on the hearts of his people. Included in the creation of a new covenant for his people was the promise, "I will forgive their wickedness and will remember their sins no more" (Jer. 31:34).

Looking back on the creation of the new covenant through the sacrifice of Jesus, Paul wrote to the Romans, "Therefore, there is now no condemnation for those who are in Christ Jesus" (Rom. 8:1). Our sin is forgiven and our guilt is removed.

But people often have one of two problems when it comes to sin and guilt, and both will keep them from reaching that place "in Christ Jesus" where sins are forgiven and condemnation is no more.

They Don't Feel Guilty

Narcissists rarely do. Psychopaths never do. People who think life is all about them and getting what they want are able to rationalize most of their guilt away. Even good folks who go to church, thinking that religion is nothing more than a means to self-improvement, a philosophy to adopt, or good advice for living a better life—can often escape the unpleasant pangs of guilt.

This chapter is not directed to such people. However, if you fall into any of those categories, you need to understand that you are lost. The Bible could not be more explicit. "All have sinned and fall short" (Rom. 3:23). And what's more, "The wages of sin is death" (Rom. 6:23).

Simply because we do not have the subjective feelings of guilt, that does not change the objective reality that every one of us is guilty before a holy God. That's why Jesus was crucified. That's why he was sent by the Father. We are all guilty. We all need to be forgiven. We all need a Savior.

Maybe you have come across this statement: "The closer you stand to the light, the bigger the shadow becomes." That's true physically and also spiritually. The closer you come to Christ, the more you will see the darkness and sin in your life and the greater will be your sense that you need his grace and forgiveness. If you feel you are living such a good and moral life that you'll be just fine when you stand before a holy God, I can assure it's not because you have done everything right. It is because you are so far from the light of Christ that you cannot see the darkness in your heart or the danger your soul is in.

We must all decide. Do we believe we will be made right with God because of the life we have lived or by the death Christ died.

One path is the way of arrogance and leads to eternal separation from God. The other is the way of humility and leads to forgiveness and reconciliation.

They Can't Accept Forgiveness

Some people live with a general sense of guilt and condemnation. Others are plagued by the thought of a particular incident that makes them feel ashamed and unworthy. In either case, they can begin to feel so condemned that they don't believe even God can forgive them. We'll talk about this more momentarily.

Sometimes people think that religions in general, and maybe Christianity in particular, try to control people with guilt and shame. They believe religion attempts to make people feel bad about themselves, and then uses that guilt to motivate people to go to church, to believe their doctrines, and to follow the rules. Faithful churches do talk about sin and guilt, but not because they want to control people. They preach on guilt because guilt is a *reality*. We all do wrong. We all choose self over others. We all at times put our will over God's. The Bible calls that sin, and sin makes us guilty. Denying our guilt doesn't set us free. It makes us disconnected from the reality of our lives. It makes us dishonest and inauthentic and spiritually sick.

Jesus taught that we should face our sins. He never spoke about guilt to make us feel worthless, but always to move us to confess our sins, experience God's grace, and make our lives right. His message was that hearts are changed and lives are transformed not by feelings of guilt but by an experience of grace. Shame and guilt may change our behavior, temporarily. But only grace and mercy change the core affections of our hearts.

Why do some people struggle to overcome their feelings of guilt? One reason may be an experience of religious abuse. You may have grown up in an overly judgmental church, or with very strict, hyper-religious parents, or under the teaching of a pastor who used Christianity in a destructive and condemning way in your life. Whatever the case, someone turned the story of God's great love for you into a message that made you feel worthless as a person, afraid of God, and ashamed of having natural desires and valid questions.

The teaching that God saw something shameful in you became embedded in your understanding of God and in your view of yourself. Years later, it's still there, making it hard to believe that God truly and deeply loves you as you are. You cannot escape the feeling that there is something wrong about you, something defective, something that God cannot accept or forgive. If that was done to you, I am sorry. You were abused and damaged by someone claiming the name of Jesus, and it breaks my heart and I'm sure it breaks God's heart too. In fact, Jesus had the sternest of words for those who caused any of his little ones to stumble (Matt. 18:6).

Another reason people struggle with guilt is they grew up in a dysfunctional, condemning family. Of course, not every dysfunctional family is condemning in nature. Some parents never correct their children, much less condemn them. They're too self-absorbed, living their own lives or too lost in their own pain to know or care what their kids are doing.

But there are some families where the parents are overbearing, the rules are unreasonable, and the punishment (verbal or physical) is harsh and demeaning. The message communicated to the children is that they can never do enough or be enough to deserve feeling good about themselves.

Parents are "God figures" to children—bigger, more powerful, and able to control their lives—so children tend to view God in the image of their parents. If a parent is always critical and never satisfied, it's easy for a child to grow into an adult who believes that nothing he or she does is ever enough to please God. The result is often a free-floating religious shame that produces constant feelings of guilt.

Some people struggle with guilt because of perfectionism. They convince themselves that they deserve respect, love, and happiness only if they do everything just right.

Perfectionism is a funny thing. It can make you feel that you are better than others and at the same time leave you feeling worse about yourself. Why? Because being so driven, you may excel at what you do, achieve more than others, and rise to the top. But because you are, in fact, imperfect—and judgmental of yourself, as perfectionists are—even if you do better than others, it's without fault, never perfect. For a perfectionist, that feels like failure, and it produces shame—yes, in our schoolwork and in our professions, but also in our relationship with God. When we think a relationship with God is about performing well enough to merit his approval, rather than experiencing the joy of being his child, how can we ever feel that we've done enough to be accepted when we know we have fallen short?

Another reason people struggle with guilt? Spiritual warfare. Now, I don't believe in a comical figure wearing red tights and carrying a pitchfork, as some folks picture the devil. But I do believe in Satan because Jesus did.

Satan has three primary forms of attack. The first is *deception*. He attempts to mislead us so that we believe wrong is right and right is wrong. In fact, we're told that the prince of darkness even presents himself as an angel of light (2 Cor. 11:14).

The devil also employs *temptation* to lead us astray. Of course, not every temptation is the work of the enemy. In fact, often we give the devil too much credit. But even Jesus was tempted by the devil in the wilderness (Matt. 4:1–11), so we can expect him to tempt us, as well (Gal. 6:1; 1 Thess. 3:5; Heb. 2:18; 4:15; James 1:14–15).

A third form of attack the Evil One uses against the children of God is *condemnation*. One of the Greek words for devil (*diabolos*) can be translated as "slanderer" or "accuser."[1] Look at the following passages:

> Now have come the salvation and the power and the kingdom of our God, and the authority of his Messiah. For the *accuser* of our brothers, who *accuses* them before our God day and night, has been hurled down. (Rev. 12:10, emphasis added)

> He showed me . . . the high priest standing before the angel of the LORD, and Satan standing at his right side to *accuse* him. (Zech. 3:1, emphasis added)

The Hebrew word we translate as "Satan" literally means "adversary" or "opponent,"[2] and indeed, he is against you. He wants you to feel condemned when you sin and unworthy of God's love when you're tempted. He will tell you that you are worthless. He will remind you that you have confessed the same sin a hundred times before. He'll sneer that if you were really a Christian, you would have stopped that sin by now. He'll whisper that you are a disappointment to your Father, that he can't possibly love you the way you are—the way you'll always be.

Why? Not because those things are true, but because it's the devil's very nature to oppose you. He is a liar and a thief and an accuser. It gives him pleasure to condemn the children of God, rob them of the joy of their salvation, and make them feel alienated from the Father who loves them. He delights in it and he's good at it. And it's something he's committed to doing.

Satan knows that if he can make you feel worthless and condemned, you'll never be bold in your witness. You may even become so discouraged that you walk away from the faith.

There's one more reason we may struggle with guilt, which we briefly touched on earlier. We've done wrong and we can't accept that God has forgiven us. Sometimes we hold on to our guilt almost as if it's a form of penance. If we don't allow ourselves to *feel* forgiven or we refuse to receive the joy that comes from being forgiven, we may endeavor to prove to God how sorry we are or try to pay for the wrong we did. But that doesn't please or honor the God who gave his Son so we could be forgiven and set free from our guilt.

If you struggle with feeling guilty, I want you to think for a moment. Is there something in particular you've done or haven't done? Have you hurt or betrayed someone? Are you plagued by the thought that you may have denied Christ? Think of what makes you feel guilty and condemned. Name it to yourself right now. It may be something that happened recently, or something you've carried for a long time. Maybe you haven't done anything wrong but instead carry an irrational guilt that is a product of the religion you grew up in or the home you grew up in or the perfectionism you live with or even the attack of the enemy. Whatever it is, name it right now.

God has a promise for you, a promise that breaks the yoke of shame and the oppression of guilt. It's a promise that sets people free: "There is now no condemnation for those who are in Christ Jesus" (Rom. 8:1).

Once you put genuine, saving faith in Christ, your status before God changes. You enjoy all the benefits that his death and resurrection bring to the believer. Among those benefits is a new identity and a relationship with a loving Father. We are no longer guilty but forgiven. We are no longer seen as sinners but as saints. We are no longer under condemnation but declared righteous in Christ (Rom. 5:1).

There is a difference between condemnation and conviction. Conviction says, "You failed." Condemnation says, "You are a failure." Conviction says, "You sinned." Condemnation says, "You're a worthless sinner." Conviction says, "You can do better." Condemnation says, "You'll never change."

If you are in Christ, God will never condemn you. The Holy Spirit will convict you of your sins. That's one of his ministries in the lives of believers. He will show you where you've failed, what you need to confess, and how you need to change. But the Spirit of God will never condemn you.

So, when you hear in your spirit, "You are a worthless failure, you'll never change, and nobody loves you," you can be sure that is *not* the voice of God. It may be the voice of a condemning parent or your own perfectionist self or the Evil One, but it is not the voice of God. When you hear such words and feel their sting, rise up in your spirit and proclaim, "But the promise of God is: there is no condemnation for those who are in Christ."

Dr. Mary Poplin is a professor at Claremont Graduate University. As a young woman she committed herself to a journey of self-discovery. She found herself attracted to radical ideologies, including postmodernism, deconstructionism, radical feminism, and Marxism. In an effort to achieve happiness and self-fulfillment, she embraced an Eastern, pantheistic New Age spirituality. She also turned to alcohol, drugs, and sexual freedom. All the while she was convinced of her own goodness.

But in certain moments, she writes, "I could see glimpses of who I really was. I was not growing freer. My heart was growing harder, my emotions darker, and my mind more confused."

One night she had a vivid dream. She found herself standing in long, seemingly endless line. She was dressed in gray, as was everyone else in the line. The sky was dark and foreboding.

Ahead she could make out a yellow light. As the line moved forward, she saw a scene reminiscent of Da Vinci's *The Last Supper*. The disciples were seated at a table, wearing beautiful colored robes. But Jesus was not with them.

In a moment she saw him in the distance, standing beside the line. When she reached Jesus, she looked into his eyes. Instantly, she felt that "every cell in my body was filled with filth." She became aware of how wasteful she had been of the life she had been given and how far away she was from all that was good and true and right.

Overcome with her guilt and shame, she could not look at Jesus any longer. She fell at his feet and began to weep. Then she felt two hands on her shoulders. His hands. Immediately she was filled with indescribable peace.

Poplin began to read the Bible, and one Sunday, sitting in a small church, she went to the altar to pray. Her prayer was simply, "Jesus, if you are real, please come and get me. Come and get me. Come and get me." And he did. She felt the same peace and acceptance that she had experienced in her dream.[3]

God wants you to know the same peace and acceptance that Mary Poplin experienced. You are forgiven. Your world does not have to be dark anymore. You do not have to be lost any longer. You do not have to be burdened by guilt and shame. I don't know who said it first, but it's true: "Jesus was crucified on the cross so you can quit crucifying yourself."

God knows it's hard for us to believe we are freed from our guilt solely by his grace. It seems too good to be true that forgiveness is something we receive, not something we must achieve. That may be why he used so many different, beautiful images in the Bible to prove it. For example, "Though your sins are like scarlet, they shall be as white as snow; though they are red as crimson, they shall be like wool" (Isa. 1:18).

Why scarlet? Why crimson? Because stains that are red are the most difficult to remove. The church I serve once had a policy: no red drinks at fellowship events or wedding receptions. Why? Because we could never get the red out of the carpet. That stain would last forever.

But God promises that the sin that has most marred and discolored your soul, the one you think you can never get out, perhaps the one you named earlier in this chapter, will be washed away and you will be white as snow.

Another passage that shows that we are free of condemnation is found in Psalm 103: "He does not treat us as our sins deserve or repay us according to our iniquities," it says. "As far as the east is from the west, so far has he removed our transgressions from us" (vv. 10, 12).

How far is the east from the west? However far you think it is—it's farther. You can always go farther east, and you can always go farther west. When God forgives your sin, that's how far he removes it from his sight.

The Greek word in the New Testament that is translated as "forgive" carries the idea of separation, putting distance between one individual and another so that they are no longer attached or associated with each other.[4] When God forgives you, he separates you from your sins in his sight. In Christ, he relates to you as if you had never sinned.

In fact, when God announced the coming of the new covenant through Isaiah, he promised, "I will forgive their wickedness and will remember their sins no more" (Jer. 31:34). Nowhere else in the Bible are we told that God has forgotten or will forget anything. Only our sins. The sin that plagues you and condemns you, the sin you think God can never forgive, he has forgotten it. If you have confessed that sin and if you have done all you can to make amends, you need to forget it too.

For several years Joe Eszterhas was the highest-paid screenwriter in Hollywood, receiving as much as $4 million per script.[5] Together his films have grossed more than $1 billion. His movies were usually dark, violent, and sexually graphic, including *Basic Instinct*, *Jagged Edge*, *Jade*, *Sliver*, and *Showgirls*. David Plotz put it well when he wrote: "Eszterhas has devoted his career to the artful composition of smut and violence."[6]

Eszterhas titled his first memoir *Hollywood Animal*, a graphic tell-all in which he described his "sexcapades" with Hollywood actresses, his copious drug consumption, and his ruthless, "take no prisoners" battles to get to the top. In an interview with the *Telegraph*, he defined the "Hollywood Animal" he had become as a man with "a complete self-absorption, absolute selfishness, a total inability to treat another human being as a human being, and an absolute fixation on success. In the process of treating everyone badly, you become inhuman yourself."[7] Simply stated, if you can think of it, Joe Eszterhas probably did it.

Wealthy, powerful, in demand, with a large home in Malibu— he had it all.

The only problem was it wasn't working.[8] He was drinking a fifth of gin and smoking four packs of cigarettes a day. He was diagnosed with throat cancer, and 80 percent of his larynx was removed. The surgeon told him the only chance he had of surviving was to stop smoking and drinking immediately.

By this time Eszterhas had realized he had become, in his own words, "cold, self-absorbed, and soulless." A month after surgery, he reached a breaking point. Jittery, trembling, angry, his entire being screamed for a drink and a cigarette. He went for a walk, unable to speak because of his operation. Bugs circled around his tracheotomy tube. Sweating and shaking, he reached the end of himself.

He fell to the curb and did something he had rarely done as a boy and never as a man. He cried. He couldn't believe it, but there were his tears, hitting the cement beside his feet. *Please God, help me. I've lived so wrong. I don't deserve it, but please forgive me. Please try to forgive me.* He couldn't speak, but in his mind and in his heart, he was praying, something he hadn't done since he was a child. This went on for five minutes, and suddenly, he stopped sweating and twitching, and he was at peace, different than he had ever felt before.

In an OnFaith article titled "My Base Instincts and God's Love," Eszterhas wrote:

Why did God save the life of a man who had trashed, lampooned, and marginalized Him most of his life? Why did He take the time and the trouble to save me? . . .

I didn't at first understand why He did. I didn't deserve His help. . . . I was unworthy. I ignore Him for forty years and then suddenly I ask Him to help me and He does? It took me some time to understand that God helped me because He loves me. Because even though we don't deserve God's love, God loves us—all of us.[9]

Joe Eszterhas has written a new tell-all. It's titled *Crossbearer: A Memoir of Faith*—because now on Sunday mornings, he is in church, leading the processional, lifting high the cross of Jesus, which brought him forgiveness and peace.

If you have put faith in Jesus, there is no condemnation, no matter what you have done. You are forgiven, and you do not honor God by feeling or acting as if you are condemned. If you have been set free, you do not glorify God by living like a slave to shame. If you have been made a new creation in Christ, you do not please God by walking around as if you are the same creature you were before you were born again. You glorify him as you lift high the cross of Jesus that saved you and carry it into the world with peace and joy.

You are not who your past says you are. You are not who your parents said you are. You are not who your sins say you are. You are not who the accuser says you are. You are who God says you are. And God says that he will not remember your sins. In Christ you are forgiven, you are accepted, and you are loved as his child.

One other passage that guarantees we are free of condemnation is found in John's first epistle. "If we confess our sins, he is faithful and just and will forgive us our sins and purify us from all unrighteousness" (1 John 1:8–9).

"If we confess our sins." That means if we admit what we have done (or haven't done), if we take responsibility for our actions and determine with God's grace to change how we live, God will forgive us. Why? Because, according to this verse, if God did not forgive us after we confessed, he would be unfaithful and unjust. But how so? Why would it be unjust if God did not forgive the sins we confess?

He would not be unjust to us. We don't deserve forgiveness. But he would be unjust and unfaithful to his Son Jesus, to the death he died and to the blood he shed on our behalf. If the death of Jesus has atoned for our sins, it would be unjust for God to demand an additional payment either from us or from his Son. He would essentially be telling Jesus, "What you did on the cross was insufficient. Something else must be added to the sacrifice you made." That is something God would never do.

But please hear this: that is exactly what we are telling Jesus when we do not accept the forgiveness he paid on the cross for our sins. We are saying, "Jesus, I do not trust that your blood is sufficient for me. I must add to the work you did on the cross. I must do some penance. I must suffer some penalty. I must pay some price because your death was not enough for me and my sins. Once I have done something more to atone for my transgressions, then I will allow myself to be forgiven."

You may be thinking, *But you don't know what I did. It was terrible. It was so wrong. It causes me pain just thinking about it.* You're right. I don't know what you did. But I know this: whatever you've done, you're not that special.

Did you murder someone? David did too. And God forgave him. Have you committed adultery? So did the woman in John 8, and Jesus forgave her. Have you denied the Lord, cursing and claiming that you didn't know him? Peter did. And Jesus forgave him. Have you persecuted Christians? Paul did, and he even put them to death. But God forgave him and used him to change the world.

The sin you are so ashamed of . . .

That thing you've hidden from everyone else . . .

The thing that makes you hate yourself and feel unworthy . . .

God knows all about it and he loves you. The truth is, if you already asked for forgiveness, then he forgave you long ago. In fact, he will remember your sin no more—that's a promise. He wants you to be free of it today.

A friend of mine had some learning disabilities that made school difficult for him as he was growing up. He felt he did not fit in with the smart kids or the athletic kids and he drifted toward the only group who would accept him—the partiers who would welcome anyone who brought enough beer or drugs to share.

The next few years were difficult for John and his family. When his parents were on their way out of the house to church, John was just getting home from an all-nighter. When he was caught with drugs, he would promise his parents he would stop using them, but he didn't. Finally, he stopped promising and feeling guilty. Instead, he became angry and defiant.

There were nights John did not come home and his parents did not know where or how he was. Rules were set and broken. Rules were reset and re-broken. But John's behavior and the consequences only got worse.

Even in his anger, John knew how much pain he was causing his parents. But that knowledge did not change his behavior; it only hardened his heart and made him angrier.

When John was arrested for possession, he was taken into custody and interrogated. After a day, he was released into his father's care. As they walked to the car together, John noticed that his father seemed weary and broken. When his father opened the door and got into the driver's seat, John climbed into the back seat. His father sat there in silence. Finally, he turned around and in a soft voice, he asked, "John, what are you doing back there?"

John shot back, "What do you think I'm doing back here? I'm waiting for you to start the car. Let's go." That's what John said, but what he felt was how badly he had let his parents down and how unworthy he was to sit beside his father.

His father got out of the car, walked to the passenger side, opened John's door, helped him out of the car as he said, "You are my son. You will always be my son. And a son's place is next to his father."

They drove home side by side and when they arrived, there was no lecture, no talk of consequences—only tears and a son embraced by two hurt but loving parents.

In that moment, John heard the voice of his heavenly Father, calling him home. His pride was broken, his anger left, his heart was changed, and his life has never been the same. The young man with the learning disability who did not fit in became a pastor, earned his doctorate, and has had a long and fruitful ministry with a heart for those who have lost their way.

If you have trusted in Christ, you are the Father's child. No matter what you have done. You belong to him and you belong with him, next to him. He does not want you burdened by guilt and shame. He does not want you to feel that you must keep your distance because you have disappointed him. He wants you to feel forgiven and loved. So he gave you a promise. "There is no condemnation for those who are in Christ Jesus." You are forgiven and you are free.

Gracious God, you know my sin and my guilt. You know how hard it has been for me to believe that I am forgiven. But I trust your promise. I trust the death your Son and my Savior died for me. I trust that the cross was sufficient for my sins. I trust that I am forgiven and that you love me and want me close to you. Because you forgive me, I forgive myself. In the name of Jesus, amen.

THREE

THE PROMISE OF NEW PURPOSE

In the previous chapter, I noted that some people think the Christian faith tries to control people with guilt and shame. A similar complaint is that Christianity has too many rules—too many "thou shalt nots" and "oh no, you don'ts." Become a Christian and you have to do all kinds of things you would rather not do and you miss out on so many things you would love to do.

No one wants a life that's little more than a long list of rules to follow. No one ever dreamed of a future with endless obligations to fulfill. We long for an adventure, a challenge, a cause that brings out our best and gives us something worth living for. Here's some good news: that's the life Jesus offers you.

One of the great privileges of my life as a pastor is hearing about the secret lives of people. When they trust you, people will reveal their hearts to you. What I have discovered is that often they are very different on the inside than they are on the outside. Around others, many folks are positive and energetic. They project an air of contentment and confidence. But when they are alone, quiet and still, they often feel worn out and weary. They wonder if they are going to make it. They're not sure what they're doing really matters. They feel no one fully understands or truly appreciates all they do. Even if they take some time off, they often do not return to their work or to their family feeling truly renewed.

Americans have more wealth, more discretionary time, and better health than at any time in history. Yet we are more stressed, depressed, and anxious than ever before. Deep down many of us feel we're missing out on life, at least what life could be.

Even if they don't know why they feel this way, most folks are sure of this: the way to the life they want is not more rules and endless to-do lists. If that's what Christianity is, they will look for life somewhere else.

Jesus made a promise to those who are tired of all the rules, who feel worn-out emotionally and spiritually, and who at the same time want an adventure to live. "Come to me, all you who are weary and burdened, and I will give you rest. Take my yoke upon you and learn from me, for I am gentle and humble in heart, and you will find rest for your souls" (Matt. 11:28–29).

To whom is Jesus speaking in this passage? People who feel weary and burdened. People who want more out of life than they're experiencing. People who wonder why everything has to be so hard and who want to be renewed in their spirits and find rest for their souls.

In Jesus' day, Jewish life was controlled by hundreds of religious laws contained in what today we refer to as the Old Testament. Just knowing all of these laws was an overwhelming task. Trying to follow them all was practically impossible. But the teachers of the Law told the people, "Obey the Law, fulfill all of its requirements, work hard enough at being righteous, prove yourself worthy, and God will accept you."

The rabbis spoke of obedience to all the Old Testament rules and regulations (more than six hundred of them) as "putting on the yoke of the Law." It was a heavy burden to carry. It was a weight that for many people transformed life from being an exciting adventure into a burdensome, soul-crushing list of have-tos and don't-evers.

What does Jesus say to those who find their existence onerous and unfulfilling? What does he offer all who wonder, *Isn't there more to life than another day of trying to follow all the rules and doing everything just right? Isn't there a way to experience joy and hope even while I'm still imperfect and broken? Isn't there some way for my life to change and the spirit inside of me to come alive?*

To all who ask these questions, Jesus says he understands and he cares. And he gives them a promise: "Come to me . . . and I will give you rest."

People are weighed down with many responsibilities and concerns. We feel responsible for the physical and emotional well-being of our children, as well as their academic success and future careers. Most of us take our vows to be thoughtful and giving spouses very seriously, and we often worry that we are not doing enough to be the husband or the wife we promised to be. We live in a capitalistic society, which has produced an incredibly high standard of living for many of us. It has also created the perception that people are only worth what they produce. So there is a constant pressure to produce more. There is little or no corporate loyalty, so many are worried about their jobs, afraid to slow down or take the time they need to recharge and enjoy the fruits of their labor.

Technology that we once thought would provide increased discretionary time now makes it possible for people to work from home. "Possible to work from home" quickly became "expected to work at home"—and to be available on the weekends and even on vacation. The wonderful little marvels that keep us connected also allow us to receive phone calls and texts in the car, at the movies, when we're at dinner with our spouses, or while spending time with our children.

As it turns out, we are always connected to our work, to world events, to anyone who has our cell number. But at the same time we feel disconnected: rarely in touch with our souls, oblivious to the beauty of nature, too distracted to hear the voice of God, often unable to focus on the person in front of us. "Always connected" has created people who are just the opposite: detached, discontented, and driven.

We place expectations upon ourselves that we should be able to handle the responsibilities and the pressures of our jobs, marriage, kids, and the rest of life on our own. Men tell themselves, "Big boys don't cry. Real men play hurt." And we sure don't talk to other men about our weaknesses, our fears, or our failures. Like Cain after he killed his brother, many of us feel condemned to walk the earth alone (Gen. 4:8–14). Women may do better than men with networking on a personal level and asking for help, but the pressures of having a successful career, presenting a socially acceptable image, often being the primary caregiver for their children, the family's social director, and a domestic architect can be overwhelming.

We may not follow the six hundred Old Testament laws, but there are unwritten laws every one of us knows. These unwritten laws tell us, "This is what you're supposed to do," "This is who you're supposed to be," and "This is how you're supposed to live."

Only, these rules don't bring joy, they don't bring peace, and they don't bring life. Just the opposite. They make us labor and they make

life a burden. What does Jesus say to men and women who are weary and burdened?

"Come to Me"

Jesus begins here because nothing is more important. Real peace, inner strength, and an abundant life—they all begin when we come to Jesus.

We look to all kinds of things outside of ourselves to bring us life and give us peace—a drink, a drug, a promotion, money, success, the admiration of others, a more attractive spouse. But our problem is not an outside problem; it's an inside problem. It's a soul problem, a spiritual problem. And there's only one reality that can satisfy what our souls long for—a relationship with the One who created us to know him.

Fifth-century theologian and philosopher Augustine, who converted to Christianity after giving in to all the desires of the flesh, wrote in his autobiography, speaking to God: "For Thou hast made us for Thyself and our hearts are restless till they rest in Thee."[1] Twelve hundred years later, Blaise Pascal wrote about the same reality, which he described as an "infinite abyss [which] cannot be filled but by an infinite and immutable object, that is, but by God himself."[2] In the early twentieth century, the Indian Christian missionary Sundar Singh described in a beautiful way the yearning of the soul and our need for a relationship with God. "In comparison with this big world, the human heart is only a small thing. Though the world is so large, it is utterly unable to satisfy this tiny heart. . . . Its capacities can only be satisfied in the infinite God. As water is restless until it reaches its level, so the soul has not peace until it rests in God."[3]

There is a reason the things of this world cannot put our souls at peace or bring our spirits alive. In Ecclesiastes we are told that God has placed eternity within the human heart (3:11). Within each of us there is a desire to be connected to what is real and true and lasting and to live for a cause that will make a difference in this world and in the world to come.

It's no surprise that trying to live by the rules does not bring rest to our souls. It's no wonder that a religion of striving to reform ourselves never satisfies our desire for an abundant life. Neither do professional success or the pleasures of the flesh make us complete or fill the emptiness within our hearts.

We are human beings made in the image of God. We have a spiritual nature. Whether we recognize it or not, the restlessness within us—the "in-here" longing we try to fulfill with an "out-there" solution—is the cry of our souls not for something, but for Someone.

One of the beauties of the Christian faith is the truth that the universe is inherently relational. Before physical reality existed, there was one God in three persons—the Father, the Son, and the Holy Spirit—sharing life together. Being made in the image of God, at the heart of who you are, there is a relational need greater than any earthly pleasure or achievement can fulfill. So, Jesus calls us to a relationship. He says, "If you want rest for your soul, first you must come to me."

David Bloom was a national debate champion in college and an avid hockey player. Type A to the max, Bloom became a highly respected journalist and an up-and-coming star as a reporter for NBC.

In 2003 Bloom was sent to cover Desert Storm and was embedded with U.S. troops as they invaded Iraq. At age thirty-nine, he was the first reporter to die during the conflict. He was not killed

in battle. He died of a pulmonary embolism, most likely caused by blood clots that formed in his legs as he traveled within the cramped confines of a U.S. tank.

His funeral was held at St. Patrick's Cathedral in Manhattan. Those who came to offer their respects included Governor Pataki, Mayor Giuliani, Tom Brokaw, Katie Couric, and Tim Russert.

Bloom had grown up in a Methodist home. But it was only a few years before his death that he came to a saving faith and a real relationship with Jesus. He started attending a Friday morning men's Bible study in New Canaan, Connecticut. Through this study and the men he met there, Bloom trusted in Jesus as his Savior and his life was changed.

Hours before his death he sent his wife, Melanie, an e-mail. In it he told her how much he loved her and his daughters and how he was looking forward to coming home. He also reflected on his life and the difference his faith had made:

I hope and pray that all my guys get out of this in one piece. But I tell you, Mel, I am at peace. Deeply saddened by the glimpses of death and destruction I have seen, but at peace with my God, and with you. I know only that my whole way of looking at life has turned upside down here. I am, supposedly at the peak of professional success, and I could frankly care less. . . . In the scheme of things it matters little compared to my relationship with you, and the girls, and Jesus. . . . When the moment comes when Jim or John or Christine or Nicole or Ava or you are talking about my last days, I am determined that they will say he was devoted to his wife and children and he gave every ounce of his being not for himself, but for those whom he cared about most, God and his family.[4]

Jesus promised, "Come to me, and I will give you rest." David Bloom came to Jesus and experienced a rest and a peace he had never known. He discovered that the promises of God are true.

Have you come to Jesus? Have you accepted him as Lord and Savior? If not, then why not do it now? Ask him to enter your life and fill the void within your soul.

If you have accepted Jesus and you are still not at peace, have you come to him with whatever it is that is burdening your soul? If not, come now; sit in his presence and pray, "Lord, here I am. Here are my labors that do not satisfy and the burdens that weigh me down. Take them from me and in their place give me what I need. Give me wisdom and strength. Give me your presence, and give me faith to hold on to your promises."

You must come honestly and openly to Jesus. You must be real with yourself and with him about your needs, your motives, your desires, your weaknesses, and your fears. Bring yourself, your real self, when you come to him.

And then sit in his presence, open your heart, and receive his Spirit. He will meet you and he will bring you peace. You may need to come to him regularly as the pressures and the fears of life weigh upon you, but he has promised that if you come to him, he will give you rest.

"Take My Yoke upon You"

After Jesus tells us to come to him, he further instructs us to put on his "yoke." The word "yoke" is a metaphor for the duties, the obligations, and the responsibilities a person takes on and commits to fulfill. In the Old Testament and in Jesus' day, good Jews took on the yoke of the Law.

We don't live under the laws of the Old Testament anymore, but we do put on yokes of various types. All of them but one weigh us down, burden our souls, and make peace impossible. Here are some that are very common.

The Yoke of the Prover

People who wear this yoke are always working to prove their own worth. They feel a need to prove something to themselves, to someone who said they'd never amount to anything, or to some voice in their head that says they must measure up and succeed. Provers feel they need to do more, achieve more, possess more, and/or be seen as more than others. Why? Because then, they are convinced, they will be worthy of respect and happiness. They are certain that once they achieve enough, they will be able to love themselves or that God and others will love them.

The problem is, no matter what the prover does, it is never enough. There is always someone who has more, does more, and is more. There is always another test to pass, another goal to attain, another weakness to overcome. There is always more to prove. So the prover is never able to rest and be at peace.

The Yoke of the Pleaser

The pleaser thinks, *If I just do enough for others to make them happy, then I'll be happy.* He or she is convinced, *If I just run myself ragged doing what others want me to do, fulfilling every request and never saying no; if I jump through enough hoops, people will love me and God will love me.*

The problem is, we were never intended to jump through hoops. We are human beings, not trained seals. We were created to be in healthy relationships founded on mutual respect and caring. Eventually pleasers feel they are being used. They quit doing tricks for the treats of applause and praise. They find themselves not at peace, but worn-out, burdened, and resentful.

The Yoke of the Rescuer

It feels good to be told, "We can't do it without you." It makes us feel important when we hear, "We've thought about it and prayed about it, and you're the only one who can do this." It makes us feel special to spot a problem and think we're the only one who can see it or who can make it right.

Whenever we put on our capes and sing, "Here I come to save the day," we feel as though we matter—until we are no longer needed and then we don't know who we are. Or until we face a problem we can't fix and then feel like failures.

The Yoke of the Selfist

This is the yoke of the person who says, "I live for me. My pleasures, my plans, and my happiness come first."

People who live for themselves usually end up by themselves, alone and miserable. When our primary goal is to be happy, we almost always discover just how wretched life can be. That's because we were made for a world whose span is bigger than a self-embrace. And if the world of a self-embrace is large enough to make a person happy, he must be a very tiny person indeed.

The yokes that are placed on us by others or that we put on ourselves all promise life and happiness. But none of them bring peace or rest. In fact, all they bring is striving, insecurity, weariness, resentment, and emptiness.

Take a moment and think deeply. Which yoke are you wearing? How did you come to take it on? What has it given you? Is it the life and the peace you desire?

The Yoke of Jesus

Before I describe this yoke, I want you to see who decides which yoke you wear. Jesus said, "Come to me . . . *Take* my yoke upon you" (emphasis added).

The choice is yours. You decide to whom you will go for life. You decide which yoke you will take on. Your childhood or a dysfunctional relationship may have led you to take on the yoke of a prover, a pleaser, a rescuer, or a selfist. Doing life right is difficult even when we are nurtured by loving relationships. But often children are raised in families where the love is conditional and they are rewarded only when they put on an inauthentic yoke and play a twisted role that serves the needs of others.

But once we say our childhood, or our circumstances, or the pain we have suffered is responsible for the lives we are living and the yokes we are wearing, we are also saying that we are *not* responsible for our lives. We give ourselves permission to be irresponsible with our lives, to become passive and complacent about where we are, and to live defeated.

You are responsible for your life, not your circumstances, not your past, not your spouse—you. You are certainly not responsible for what has been done to you, but you are responsible for how you move forward in life. Believe that; claim that; be responsible for that. You are a human being. You are the most resourceful and creative being God has brought into existence. You have the ability to make decisions that will overcome your past, change your present, and lead to a future that is good and full. You can choose to wear a yoke different from the one life has placed upon you. With God's help you can recognize that the yoke you have been wearing has only made life a labor and a burden. And you can choose to replace that yoke with the one that will bring you rest—the yoke of Jesus.

What is the yoke that Jesus offers us? Stated simply, the yoke of Jesus is a yoke of love, of relationship.

When Jesus was asked which commandment is the greatest, he replied that the greatest commandment is to love God with our whole being, and the next is to love our neighbor as ourselves. Then he said, "All the Law and the Prophets hang on these two command-ments" (Matt. 22:36–40). The reason for the six hundred–plus laws that made up the yoke of the Old Testament and all the teaching of the prophets is love. That's all that God has ever asked us to do—love him faithfully and love others sacrificially. Love is the yoke God calls us to take on.

When we understand that life is about love, everything changes. Life is transformed from a burden to bear, with endless boxes to check, into an adventure of opening our hearts to God and others. Serving becomes less of a burden and more of a joy. In the process, we are changed.

Mort Kondracke has had an illustrative career in the world of journalism. Among other positions, Kondracke was the *Chicago Sun-Times* White House correspondent, a regular on *The McLaughlin Group*, the Washington Bureau chief for *Newsweek*, and the executive editor for *Roll Call* for twenty years.

His book *Saving Milly* chronicles his life with his wife, especially the years after Milly was diagnosed with Parkinson's disease.

In the book he describes how for most of their marriage he had lived primarily for himself, for his career, and for the success he was driven to achieve. Kondracke is honest in detailing how often he ignored his wife and his children.

He also writes how Milly helped him when it became obvious that he had a problem with alcohol. It was her influence that got him to AA and ultimately to sobriety.

The first sign of Milly's Parkinson's was trouble with signing her name. Walking became difficult and then impossible. Her speech became garbled. Her deterioration continued to the point that eating and drinking became problematic. Eventually she was unable to turn over in bed by herself. Finally, she was no longer able to control her most basic bodily functions.

In the book Kondracke writes about his journey of learning to love another person. How hard it was at first to slow down and spend time with Milly, to talk to her and to stroke her face when she couldn't respond. How difficult it was to put her needs above his own—to bathe her, to feed her, to reach in and pull food out of her throat when it got stuck there, to change her soiled clothing. And then the surprising realization that he was no longer doing these things as an obligation. They were no longer difficult or distasteful. They no longer felt like a sacrifice he was making for someone else. They felt like love.

Often during this time, his career on hold, Kondracke spent time praying for Milly but also for himself, "God, what is my purpose here on earth?" He writes that he had expected some grand mission, but every time he prayed, he got the same answer, "Take care of Milly."

In an interview in *Christianity Today*, Kondracke said, "So that's what I did. And in the process I've become a different, better person—someone I never expected to be."[5]

Rules and following the law can control our outer behavior but they cannot make us better people because they do not transform our hearts. Love does for us what the yokes of the world can never do. Love changes us. It comforts and helps the people we love, sure. But it changes us. It clarifies our purpose and simplifies our life. Even in the midst of pain and loss and grief, love brings peace. And it makes us different, better—more like our rabbi Jesus.

Love does not make our lives easy. It does not cause us to do less, but more for God and for others. But it does bring joy and peace. That's because the yoke of love grounds us in what is real, valuable, and eternal—exactly what the spirits within us yearn for. There is eternity within our hearts. We long to live for something that is so real that it will always exist. The best I can tell from the Scriptures, when this world is gone, what will remain forever are God and people. So our lives must be lived loving God and others. Nothing else will bring real fulfillment or the rest we long to know. The other yokes we put upon ourselves bring striving and weariness. The yoke of Jesus brings peace and rest.

I know "loving God and others" is a bit nebulous. Let's simplify it. This week, each day, intentionally do one act that expresses your love to God and do one thing to bring love into the life of another person.

How do we love God? Spend some time with him. Pray. Listen to a praise song or a great hymn, and then tell God what he means to you. Take a short walk and let God know that you want more of him in your life. Make a special gift to help the poor. List all the blessings you are grateful for and thank God for being so good to you. Go on a mission trip, or get involved with a ministry at your church.

How do we love someone else? Think of someone who is going through a tough time and send a card, write an e-mail, or make a phone call. Take him or her to lunch and ask how that friend is doing. Pray for someone. Spend a few minutes extra listening to someone, and look at that person as if you are genuinely interested in what he or she has to say. Do a chore for a neighbor. Invite someone to church or to Bible study. Tell your spouse how much he or she means to you. Compliment someone at work, but give it enough thought that your words are personal and fitting, more than a compliment— a blessing. Thank someone who made your life better recently or in the past.

Love God and love our neighbor. That is the yoke of Jesus. That is the life we are called to live. That is the life that will cause us to thrive and that will bring us peace.

"Learn from Me"

Jesus will teach us how to live in love—if we're willing. The life we are called to live is a learning process. We won't always get it right. We'll make mistakes. That's what learners do.

When a disciple followed a rabbi, the main goal was not simply to learn what the rabbi knew. The disciple's intention was to learn to live how the rabbi lived. The disciple wanted to see the world the way his rabbi did, relate to people the way his rabbi did, respond to problems and know God the way his rabbi did. When a young man committed himself to following a rabbi and learning his way of life, it was referred to as putting on that rabbi's yoke.

We are called to follow a Rabbi and we are called to learn his way of life. Do we need to fear when we fail? No. Because our Rabbi tells us that he is "gentle and humble in heart" (Matt. 11:29). Jesus is not a harsh judge but a gentle encourager. He will be understanding and kind with our failings. He will embrace us when we fail. He will be patient as we learn the way of love.

Look how Jesus ends his promise: "You will find rest for your souls. For my yoke is easy and my burden is light" (Matt. 11:29–30).

"Easy" in this verse means "well fitting." "The life I call you to," Jesus says, "you were made for it, and it was made for you."

"My burden is light." Jesus says, "I am not in your life to make it difficult or arduous. I'm not here to give you more rules or a long list of have-tos that will weigh you down and take life from you, leaving you weary and demoralized. Loving God and loving others—it fits you because you were made to love."

Clayton Christensen is the Kim B. Clark professor of business administration at the Harvard Business School. He has founded two investment and consulting companies, authored nine books, and was ranked first in the Thinkers50, the global ranking of business leaders created by Des Dearlove and Stuart Crainer.[6] In 2010 Christensen was diagnosed with cancer, and later that year he wrote a piece for the *Harvard Business Review*. He concludes his article:

> My ideas have generated enormous revenue for companies that have used my research. But as I've confronted this disease, it's been interesting to see how unimportant that impact is to me now. I've concluded that the metric by which God will assess my life isn't dollars but the individual people whose lives I've touched. Don't worry about the level of individual prominence you have achieved; worry about the individuals you have helped become better people. Think about the metric by which your life will be judged, and make a resolution to live every day so that in the end, your life will be judged a success.[7]

It should not take a cancer diagnosis or a brush with death to show us what is most important. We were made to love. We were made to serve God and others. When we put down the other yokes we have carried and we learn to live in love, we will each become someone we never expected but always wanted to be. And we will find rest for our weary souls.

———————————

Lord Jesus, I give you the yokes I have worn in the past. They have made my life a burden and they have made my spirit weary. I come to you now because I want you. Not more rules, not a list of good things to do, not a religion about you. I want you. I want to know you. I want to be like you. I want to live in love the way you did. Teach me your way of life, and place upon my shoulders your yoke, which is easy and brings peace. In the name of Jesus, amen.

———————————

FOUR
THE PROMISE OF CONSTANT PRESENCE

Whatever you have done, God is for you. Wherever you have wandered, God is with you. However you have failed, God still wants you. No matter how lost and alone you feel, God has not forsaken you. Regardless of how far you run, you will find him waiting there for you.

God loves you. He is committed to you. And he gives you this promise: "I will always be with you—I will never leave or forsake you."

God makes this promise in many different places in Scripture. In the Old Testament, he spoke to his people through Moses, saying, "The LORD your God goes with you; he will never leave you nor forsake you" (Deut. 31:6). In the New Testament, the last words of Jesus in the book of Matthew are, "Surely I am with you always, to the very end of the age" (28:20).

The Scriptures teach that when we are certain of nothing else, we can always be sure that God is with us. We can face life with confidence and courage, certain that greater is he that is in us than he that is in the world (1 John 4:4). It was this certainty that allowed David to write, "Even though I walk through the darkest valley, I will fear no evil, for you are with me; your rod and your staff, they comfort me" (Ps. 23:4).

Velma Griffin had a dear face with a broad smile. Well into her eighties, she moved slowly but had a quick wit. Her hair was gray, cut short, with just a little curl. I liked Velma, and for some strange reason she loved me.

Velma became ill. Really, she just started to wear out. She was taken to the hospital in hopes that she might recover. At first she could sit up, eat, and make a little joke whenever I entered her room. But as the weeks passed, she became weaker and weaker. Finally she couldn't lift her head and had to be fed through a tube.

Velma was pretty much alone. She had never had children. Her husband had been dead for many years. Her two or three living friends were frail and could not get to the hospital to see her.

Only a few days before her death, Velma had a particularly bad night. Her breathing stopped over and over. The next morning the nurse told me what had happened and said, "We thought we had lost her for sure, but she's a little better now."

I entered her room, knelt beside her bed, looked into her eyes, and pretended to scold her. "Velma, you gave us quite a scare last night. You even frightened the doctors. I want you to stop that."

Did I tell you that Velma was a Christian? Not a Sunday-morning-go-to-church Christian, but a woman who knew Jesus and walked with him as if he were her best friend.

She whispered to me, "Well, I'm sorry if you were scared, but I wasn't."

"Oh no?" I said. "What makes you so brave?"

She answered, "'For I the LORD thy God will hold thy right hand, saying unto thee, Fear not; I will help thee'" (Isa. 41:13 KJV). Then she said: "He was here with me the whole time."

That night Velma looked death right in the face and it didn't frighten her at all.

No one beside her bed. No one to hold her hand. No one to say, "It's okay, dear. I'm right here with you." It would have been so easy for Velma to be afraid, but she wasn't. The only way I can explain it is the promises of God are unfailing, and the One who said, "I will never leave you nor forsake you" is true to his word.

"I will be with you." It's a simple, but profound statement. What does it mean that God is with us? To begin with, *God is concerned about our lives and is committed to our well-being.*

Many people stumble over the truth claims of the Christian faith. They find them hard to accept. For many, it is difficult to even believe there is a God. You cannot see him or touch him. You cannot conduct a scientific study or crank him into a mathematical formula and prove his existence. A God who is beyond our senses—that's a real stumbling block for some people.

Another tough-to-understand claim is that Jesus was God incarnate. Two natures—one divine and one human—in the same person. How such a thing could be is not easy to comprehend, much less believe.

Of course, there's the resurrection. Jesus was truly crucified, dead, and buried. On the third day, he rose from the dead. Some people simply cannot accept that such a thing is possible.

But there's another cardinal doctrine of the Christian faith that I find more challenging to believe than the existence of God, or the divinity of Christ, or the resurrection of Jesus from the dead. It's this: God knows *me* and he loves *me*. He cares about *me*, and he wants a relationship with *me*.

Scientists estimate that the known universe is 92 billion light-years in diameter.[1] That means a beam of light traveling at 186,000 miles per second would require 92 billion years to travel from one edge of the known universe to the other. The universe is believed to contain at least 100 billion galaxies with a total of roughly 70 billion trillion stars.[2] Revolving around one of these stars, is a small planet, and on it are 7 billion human beings. It makes us wonder even more than the psalmist did, "What is man, that thou art mindful of him?" (Ps. 8:4 KJV).

Yet the Christian faith teaches that God knows and cares about each one of us. Personally, I find that infinitely more difficult to conceive than God raising Jesus from the grave. The great Christian mind of G. K. Chesterton put it this way: "All men matter. You matter. I matter. It's the hardest thing in theology to believe."[3]

You matter to the God of the universe. He knows you. He loves you. He promises that he will be with you and will never forsake you. He is so concerned about you and your well-being that his Word tells you to "cast all your anxiety on him because he cares for you" (1 Peter 5:7).

God knows your hurts. He knows your fears. He knows why you are anxious and worried. He knows how you struggle to do what's right and how bad you feel when you do wrong. And he wants you to cast your cares on him because he cares for you.

When our sons were young, I would play a game with them. I would look at one of them and ask, "Boy, does your daddy love you?" He would say yes or nod his head. Then I would ask, "Does your daddy love you because you are handsome?" He would reply no. I'd press on. "Does your daddy love you because you are smart?" Again, he would answer no. "Does your daddy love you because you are good?" Once more he would respond no. "That's right," I'd say. "Your daddy does not love you because you are handsome, or smart, or good. I love you because you are mine and you will always be mine and I will always love you."

Why does your Father love you? Because you are his and you will always be his and he will always love you.

Through the prophet Isaiah, God expressed the depth of his commitment to us. "Can a mother forget the baby at her breast and have no compassion on the child she has borne? Though she may forget, I will not forget you! See, I have engraved you on the palms of my hands" (Isa. 49:15–16).

What would it take for a mother to forget the child she'd once carried and nursed? The child she dreamed of and prayed for before he or she was ever born. The child she rocked to sleep at night and cared for when he or she was sick. The child that has brought her more joy than any material possession or earthly accomplishment. What would be required for a loving mother to walk away from her child and stop caring?

God is saying, through the prophet Isaiah, "Should you ever make such a mess of your life, do so much wrong, and become such a disappointment that your mother would abandon you and say, 'I no longer have a child,' even then *I* will not leave you or forsake you." Your Father loves you not because you are handsome or smart or good. Not because you do everything right or always make him proud. He loves you because you are his, and he will never forsake you.

The Isaiah passage ends with God saying, "See, I have engraved you on the palms of my hands." That means even more to us than it did to Isaiah because we know the manner in which our names were written upon the palms of our Savior: spikes were driven through his hands when he was crucified. When the risen Christ appeared to his disciples, he made certain they looked at the wounds still there in his hands. And we know that even today, glorious in heaven, Jesus still bears the marks of his love where our names are inscribed and will remain forever.

As human beings, we suffer great hurts, and when we do, we sometimes wonder if God has abandoned us. We make huge mistakes, and it is natural to think—to fear, really—that maybe God has given up on us. But God has promised, "'Never will I leave you; never will I forsake you.' So we say with confidence, 'The Lord is my helper; I will not be afraid'" (Heb. 13:5–6).

Life will be unfair to you. It will cause you to suffer physically and emotionally. It will shatter your dreams and leave you confused. There will come a time when you find yourself desperate for answers that make sense out of the chaos your life has become. But in the midst of your pain and your confusion, never let life take away from you the certainty that God knows you, he cares for you, and he is committed to you. You are not alone. You never have been and you never will be. The Lord is with you. He is concerned about you and committed to you.

When we say God is with us, we also mean *God understands us and the problems we face.* Over the years I have spoken with scores of people who were struggling to overcome the pain they experienced as children. Some have suffered abuse—physical, emotional, or sexual. Others have suffered wounds of absence—a parent was missing in the child's life because of death, divorce, drugs or alcoholism, imprisonment, or work. The complaint I have heard most about fathers is this: "I felt like I never knew my father, and that he never knew me." This can occur in a child's life even when the father is physically present if he is unwilling to or incapable of listening to his child and understanding his or her hopes and struggles and fears.

A child wants to be seen, wants to be known. What does a little boy say when he rides his bike past his parents for the first time? "Hey, look at me!" What does a young girl say when she is finally able to do a cartwheel after trying over and over? "Mommy, Daddy, look what I can do."

When a parent takes the time to look at us, we feel valued. When a mom takes the time to listen to us, we feel we matter. When a dad does the hard work of understanding who we are, what is important to us, and how we see the world, we feel we are not alone because someone cares.

In the Old Testament, we were given a promise. "The Lord himself will give you a sign: The virgin will conceive and give birth to a son, and will call him Immanuel" (Isa. 7:14). "Immanuel" means "God with us."

In Jesus, God fulfilled his promise and became Immanuel, God with us. In fact, he came to be one of us. Paul wrote of the incarnation of Jesus, "He made himself nothing by taking the very nature of a servant, being made in human likeness" (Phil. 2:7). In commenting on this verse and the Greek word for "likeness" used here (*homoiwmati*), Professor Johannes Schneider explains the depth to which God was willing to "be with us" in Christ: "He truly became man, not merely in outward appearance, but in thought and feeling. He who was the full image of God became the full image of man."[4]

One of the earliest heresies that beset the church was Docetism. The name comes from a Greek word that means "to seem" or "to appear." The belief was that Jesus only seemed to be a man; he only appeared to have a body, because God would never condescend to become so intimately connected to his creation. The idea that God would become human was scandalous.

But that is what happened with the coming of Christ. "The Word became flesh and made his dwelling among us" (John 1:14). He took on our nature—our flesh, our thoughts, our feelings, and our ability to be hurt and to suffer. That means God has lived where we live, how we live. That means he understands you and me.

Does God understand the pain you feel when you are betrayed by a friend or deserted by those you love? Yes, because Jesus was betrayed and deserted. Does God understand when you give your heart, only to be rejected? Does he understand what it's like to be misrepresented and to be lied about? Has he ever felt what it's like to be mocked and taunted and scorned? Yes, because in Jesus, God was with us, living where we live, being tempted as we are tempted, and suffering how we suffer. You are not alone. God understands you, your struggles, and your pain.

Edward Shillito was an infantryman who survived the trench warfare of World War I and who later became a clergyman. His poem "Jesus of the Scars" captures how desperately we need a God who is with us and how healing it is to know that God understands how difficult and excruciating human life can be.

> If we have never sought, we seek Thee now;
> Thine eyes burn through the dark, our only stars;
> We must have sight of thorn-pricks on Thy brow,
> We must have Thee, O Jesus of the Scars.
>
> The heavens frighten us; they are too calm;
> In all the universe we have no place.
> Our wounds are hurting us; where is the balm?
> Lord Jesus, by Thy Scars, we claim Thy grace.

The other gods were strong; but Thou wast weak;
They rode, but Thou didst stumble to a throne;
But to our wounds only God's wounds can speak,
And not a god has wounds, but Thou alone.[5]

Our God, no other God but our God, has scars. That means he is with us. He has lived where we lived, struggled as we struggle, and suffered as we suffer.

The author of Hebrews wrote,

For we do not have a high priest who is unable to empathize with our weaknesses, but we have one who has been tempted in every way, just as we are—yet he did not sin. Let us then approach God's throne of grace with confidence, so that we may receive mercy and find grace to help us in our time of need (Heb. 4:15–16).

"Hey, God, look at me." He has. "Listen to the cries of my heart." He has. "Understand me." He does. "Tell me I'm not alone." *You're not.*

God is with you. When you scream in frustration, when you cry at night, when you feel that the entire world is against you, he is with you. He is not a high priest who is unable to empathize with your weakness and your pain. He is with you; he knows you; he understands you. He is present to give you mercy and grace in your time of need.

When we say that God is with us, we also mean *God is working for our good.*

Whether we can see what God is doing or not, we can be sure that God is committed to making our lives good and full.

No man did more to spread the gospel in the first century than Paul, and no man suffered more for being faithful to his calling. Five times Paul was given thirty-nine lashes, three times he was beaten with rods, three times he was shipwrecked, once he was stoned by an angry mob and left for dead, and on many occasions he went without sufficient food, water, and even clothing. Still he wrote, "We know that in all things God works for the good of those who love him, who have been called according to his purpose" (Rom. 8:28).

Paul did not write that everything that happens to us is good. But he does say that in every situation God is present and working on our behalf.

We Americans are terribly materialistic, and our theology tends to be rather shallow. Consequently, we may think that "working for our good" means that God is engineering a future for us that is trouble-free, financially blessed, and devoid of suffering. But that is not "the good life" God promises us, nor is that how the Scriptures define what's best for us. The good life that God offers us is a life where we are becoming more like Jesus and being used for a great and godly purpose.

God's great goal for each of us is that we become "conformed to the image of his Son" (Rom. 8:29). What was Jesus like? He was patient. How do we learn patience? There's only one way: people irritate us over and over and we learn to remain calm and loving. Jesus was forgiving. How do we become forgiving? We are sinned against, treated unfairly, and hurt deeply, and we learn to let it go. Jesus was faithful. How do we become faithful? We face situations that fill us with fear and require us to sacrifice something we hold dear, and still we do what God is calling us to do. A trouble-free life that is devoid of great challenges and real suffering does not, cannot, create a Christlike character.

When God is working for our good, he is working to create a Christlike character within us. He is working to transform us into people who love what Jesus loved, think as Jesus thought, and serve how Jesus served. Jesus' life was not trouble-free, devoid of stress, or without suffering. It was difficult and draining and costly because he lived to bring the kingdom of God into the lives of others. He is our model of the good life, not the picture painted by television preachers who describe God's favor as material abundance and special treatment by others.

Through the men's ministry of our church, I speak to five hundred men weekly. I got their attention one morning when I told them I was going to do many of their funerals. "You're going to die," I said, "and you're going to be in a box in our chapel, and I'm going to be the guy to speak on your behalf. When that day comes, it's going to be my job to make you look like a good person. And before that day comes, it's your job to give me some decent material to work with!"

I went on: "You had better leave me with more than you loved golf, you liked to travel, you enjoyed nature (which in Texas means you liked to shoot things), and you were a big supporter of your college's football team. I don't mind stretching the truth at funerals. I've done it before and I'll do it again. If need be, I'll do it for you. But it's really distasteful when I have to get up there and lie. And that's exactly what I'll have to do if that's all you leave me with even if you were in church every week, you were fun to hang out with, and we were friends."

I have conducted 231 funerals. More than two hundred times, I have sat in a kitchen or a living room with family members, and I have asked them, "Tell me what was best about your loved one. What will you remember and cherish forever?" And not once has anyone said, "He made a lot of money" or "She wore the finest clothes." Neither has anyone said, "He drove the coolest cars," or "She traveled to the most exotic places." No one has even said, "He was a great success at work," not when I asked, "What was best about your loved one?"

No, at the end of a life, when people think about what matters and what makes a life worth living, they talk about giving. They talk about sacrifice. They talk about putting others first and yourself second. They talk about paying a price to do what's right, being faithful when it was painful, and being willing to suffer so others will be blessed.

"Rob, tell people that when my father died, my mother got a job, worked all day, came home tired, cooked for us, and helped with our homework. She went without anything for herself for years so we could dress like the other kids and go on the same trips as everyone else. Tell folks that no one ever had a more giving, loving mother."

"Tell people that Dad worked two jobs so we could go to college."

"Be sure and say that my brother gave up a huge promotion because his kids were struggling and he didn't think it was the right time to move them."

"Let people know that my wife was the kindest, most encouraging woman any man could be married to—and that the only reason I was as successful at work is because she believed in me and supported me."

"Tell them that my father's greatest joy was seeing the look on the faces of the families he built Habitat for Humanity homes for."

Those are the things people tell me when they stop and search their hearts and come up with an answer to the question, What was best about your loved one? What made his or her life matter?

Please understand this. You can have an easy life or you can have a great life. You can have a comfortable life or you can have a glorious life. If you decide that God's best for you is a life that is easy, comfortable, and trouble-free, you are going to make some poor pastor's job awfully tough when your day comes. Worse yet, you will have wasted the life God gave you.

Pat Tillman turned down a $3.6 million contract and left his professional football career with the Arizona Cardinals in the aftermath of 9/11. He enlisted in the United States Army to fight terror and oppression. He became an army ranger and served several tours in combat before he died in the mountains of Afghanistan. (Sadly, his death was the result of friendly fire.) In his journal he wrote, "Sometimes my need to love hurts . . . Is there a cure? Of course. But I refuse. Refuse to stop loving, to stop caring. To avoid those tears, that pain. . . . To err on the side of passion is human and right and the only way I'll live."[6]

Tillman by all accounts was not a believer. But he understood more about the good life God has for us than many who claim the name of Jesus. Seeing the world and its problems and not caring, not weeping, not stepping up to help—that is not being Christlike and that is not the life God calls us to live. None of us ever looked forward to living that kind of life. None of us ever dreamed of a day when we would be all grown up and not feel deeply for others or sacrifice for what we say we believe. God's best life for us is not being free of the world and its problems but being compelled to care for the world and its problems. That's who Jesus was, and God's best for us is becoming like him.

The promise that God is working for our good is not the promise of a trouble-free life. In fact, Jesus promised his disciples the opposite: "In this world you will have trouble" (John 16:33). What we are promised is that God will be with us, working for our good, making us more like Jesus, and giving us opportunities to do his work in the world.

There will be times when you cannot see God at work. You may not sense his presence in your life. It may seem that your prayers go unanswered. You may feel like the man who was brought by a friend to our prayer team after a Sunday service. He had suffered with cancer for many years. When we asked him if he knew that God loved him, he whispered, "I don't think God even knows my name anymore." In those moments, hold on to the promise of God. He is with you. He is working for your good.

There was a day when God seemed far away. An innocent life that had always been faithful was nailed to a cross. A beautiful man who had done nothing but love writhed in pain. Evil men mocked his suffering and called him a fool. As he died and his body was placed in a tomb, everyone who had believed in his words and trusted his promises lost all hope and wondered how life could ever be good again. The heavens became dark, and people wondered, "Where is God?"

Today we know where God was. He was there—in that moment, on that cross, in the midst of that suffering. He was there overcoming evil, bringing good out of bad, accomplishing a work on our behalf that would change the world and give us life.

Never doubt that God is with you, working for your good. In the darkness, in your suffering, in your confusion, he is with you.

When American author and poet Edgar Guest was a young man, his first child died. That night, as he grieved the loss of his baby, Guest wrote that he felt lonely and defeated. There seemed to be nothing in life ahead of him that mattered or was worth living for.

The next morning he went to his neighborhood drugstore. The druggist motioned for Guest to follow him into a small office in the back of the store and shut the door behind them. The man put both hands on Guest's shoulders and said, "Eddie, I can't really express what I want to say, the sympathy I have in my heart for you. All I can say is that I'm sorry. And I want you to know that if you need anything at all, I want you to come to me. What is mine is yours."

Years later Guest wrote, "Just a neighbor across the way—a passing acquaintance. Jim Potter may have long since forgotten that moment when he gave me his hand and his sympathy, but I shall never forget it—never in all my life. To me it stands out like the silhouette of a lonely tree against a crimson sunset."[7]

Never forget the lonely tree where Jesus stretched out both his hands. It is the silhouette of a promise that will give you strength for today and hope for tomorrow. You are not alone. He is there. Wherever you are, he is with you.

Whatever you need, you can come to him. He is with you, working to heal your heart, give you strength, and bring good into your life.

———————

God who came to be with us in Jesus Christ, I confess I often listen to my feelings more than I listen to your voice. My feelings tell me that I am alone. Your promise tells me that you are with me. My feelings tell me that my problems are overwhelming and that hope is gone. Your Word tells me that you are my helper and I have no reason to be afraid. My feelings tell me that my life is going nowhere. You tell me that in all things you are working for my good. I choose to trust you. I will believe your Word. I will stand on your promises because my feelings come and go, but your promises are unfailing. In Jesus' name, amen.

———————

FIVE

THE PROMISE OF LOVING GUIDANCE

Of all the questions Christians ask, two of the most frequent are: What is God's will for my life? and, How can I know what God's will is?

You may be a young adult, wondering what to do with the rest of your life. You may be a mother who has poured your life into your children, but they have left home and you struggle to know what's next. Maybe you are in an unhappy marriage or you hate your job, and you know you cannot accept the way things are, but you are unsure how to move forward. Possibly, you have just gone through a divorce or you have recently retired. What now? You may have been done terribly wrong, and you wonder, *Do I need to confront the person who hurt me, or simply forgive and let it go?* There will be many times in our lives when we find ourselves asking the question: How can I know what God's will is for me?

God will guide you. It's a promise we find often in the Scriptures, nowhere more clearly than in the book of Proverbs. "Trust in the LORD with all thine heart; and lean not unto thine own understanding. In all thy ways acknowledge him, and he shall direct thy paths" (Prov. 3:5–6 KJV).

The promise is not that God will tell us exactly what to do in every situation. The promise is not that we will never be in doubt about what his will is. The promise is not that we will always feel his presence or clearly understand his plan. The promise is that God will direct our paths—he will lead us in ways that are righteous and that will bring us into the abundant life we are promised in Christ.

It is important to recognize that God's promise to guide us in Proverbs 3 is conditional. There are certain conditions, certain prerequisites we must fulfill for God to lead us into the fullness of his will. But if we do our part, we can be certain that God will direct our steps and guide us throughout our lives.

What must we do for God to lead us into his will? First, "trust in the LORD with all your heart." This means we must decide to obey God's will even before we know what God's will is. God is not in the business of laying out his plans for our lives so we can mull them over and decide whether they suit us or not. If you want to know God's will so you can make it nothing more than one more alternative to consider, then do not expect to hear from God. If you want to be guided by God, you must decide before you know God's plan that if he makes it known to you, you will do his will.

We have all been told, "Never sign a contract without reading the fine print" and "Never sign a check until the amount has been filled in." Why? Because if we commit ourselves before we know what the commitment is, we may find ourselves committed to a lot more than we can handle. When it comes to business and to finances, it makes perfectly good sense not to commit to something until we know exactly what that something is.

But with God, it's just the opposite. In John 7, Jesus is speaking to people who are skeptical about his teaching. Was he a false teacher, leading people into error? Or had he come from heaven with a revelation about God's will that was right and true? How did Jesus respond? "Anyone who chooses to do the will of God will find out whether my teaching comes from God or whether I speak on my own" (John 7:17).

Do you see the pattern? Jesus says, first we must decide to do God's will. Then we will be able to recognize what his will is. Learning God's will is not some mental exercise, where we write down all our options and then determine which one is the most pleasing or makes the most sense to us. No, we trust the Lord with all our hearts first. Then he will guide us. And part of trusting in the Lord is agreeing to walk in his ways even before we know what his ways are.

Why can we trust God before we know what his will is? Two important reasons. One, *God is omniscient.* He knows all that can be known. We see a small part of the world; God sees everything. We struggle to understand the situation we are facing; God comprehends all that is. We don't know what tomorrow may bring. God holds eternity in his hand.

James reminds us to be humble in our planning, given how little we know. "Now listen, you who say, 'Today or tomorrow we will go to this or that city, spend a year there, carry on business and make money.' Why, you do not even know what will happen tomorrow" (James 4:13–14). Contrast our limitations with the knowledge of God. "To God belong wisdom and power; counsel and understanding are his" (Job 12:13).

Who should I trust to know what's best for me? Myself with my limited understanding, often bewildered by the events of the day and absolutely incapable of predicting what will happen tomorrow? Or the omniscient God, who knows all that is, including what is best for me?

Not only can we trust God because he is all-knowing; we can trust him because *God is good*. Jesus described God as a gracious Father who finds joy in bringing good gifts into the lives of his children (Matt. 7:9–11). "If God is for us, who can be against us?" Paul asked. "He who did not spare his own Son, but gave him up for us all—how will he not also, along with him, graciously give us all things?" (Rom. 8:31–32). God loves us. He wants only what is good for us. He delights in bringing blessing into our lives.

We can trust God with our lives because he is both wise and good. If he were only wise, we might not trust him because we could not be sure that his heart is kind. If all we knew about God is that he is good, we might not trust him because he might not know what is best for us. But he is both wise and good. He knows what is best for us and he wants what is best for us. We can trust in the Lord with all our hearts and agree to be obedient to his will even before we know what that will is. His paths for us might not always be easy or pleasant, but they will always be good and right.

In preparing for a lecture on the passage in 2 Timothy 2 where Paul compares the Christian life to the life of an athlete, I had a decision to make. Should I use my rather extensive experience of sitting on a Little League bench until we were sufficiently ahead or so far behind that putting me into right field would make no difference to the outcome of the game to explain the passage? Or should I ask three very successful coaches I knew what qualities they believed were necessary to be a successful athlete?

I reached out to the coaches, and though they used different words, they all listed the same traits. The player must have some natural, God-given ability. He (they all coached boys) must be willing to work hard to perfect his skills. He must be able to focus on the moment, not distracted by the mistake he had just made or worried about something that might happen later in the game. And truly great athletes possess a ferociously competitive spirit.

It was one final trait that I found fascinating. All three coaches described it as essential. They said the athlete must be teachable. They had all tried to coach athletes with great potential but who would not listen to them and who were not open to advice and correction. The result was that they never experienced the level of success they might have enjoyed.

Curious, I asked, "What does it take to be teachable?" The answer was as simple as it was profound. "The athlete has to trust us. The athlete must believe the coach knows what's best for him and wants what's best for him. If he doesn't, he'll fight us, he won't do what we tell him to, he won't learn what he needs to know, and, ultimately, he will find himself in a game lost, not knowing where he is or what he is supposed to do. And he will not succeed."

If we are to succeed in life, we must decide now that God can be trusted. We must decide that when God shows us his will, we will trust him with all of our hearts and obey what he tells us to do whether we understand his plan or not. Why? Because God knows what is best for us and because God wants what is best for us.

Another prerequisite to walking in God's will is "lean not on your own understanding." In other words, we must humble ourselves.

We find this same truth in the Psalms. "He guides the humble in what is right and teaches them his way" (25:9).

Humility says, "I don't have all the answers. I don't always know what to do. Many times in the past when I was sure I was right, I could not have been more wrong. So I will look for wisdom that is greater than my own."

This is fairly easy for me because I'm pretty much an idiot when it comes to anything practical or manly. Sports, parallel parking, repairs around the house, figuring out how something works, and by "something" I mean anything; I am utterly hopeless. The honest truth is that I do not even know where the hammer is in our house, and if I asked my wife, she would want to know what I was planning to do with it before she told me where I could find it.

Worst of all is my sense of direction. Evidently, some part of the human brain that other people possess is missing from mine. Indoors or outdoors, whether I've made the trip before our not, it makes no difference. I am going to make a wrong turn and get lost at some point.

My wife, Peggy, and I have been married for forty years. One time I've been right about directions and she's been wrong. We were driving in the Mexican desert and she had been asleep for two hours. She woke up and said, "I think we're going the wrong way." I told her she was mistaken and that I was sure we were on course.

And I was right. That happened more than thirty years ago and I remember it because it is the only time in four decades I have ever been right and she has been wrong about directions.

The only way I have ever been right when I was uncertain which way to go was to become very still, take a deep breath, listen to the little voice inside my head—and do the exact opposite. I am not joking. That is the method I used to find my way around before I got an iPhone.

Do you think it's hard for me to take directions from Peggy? Well, yes and no. Yes, because I have to swallow my pride, admit how inept I am, and ask for help. But no, it's not hard because I don't want to drive around lost half my life, and I know she can help me.

Being so lost at so many things in life, knowing how little I know, learning over time how easily I make things about me when they're not, how often I let my emotions cloud my judgment, how often I have been certain I was in the right only to learn later how absolutely wrong I was—do you think I'm going to trust in my own understanding? No, I may be an idiot, but I'm not stupid.

When it comes to more important matters than driving around town or repairing a loose door handle; when it comes to how I should live my life, how I can best help my family, and how I should conduct my ministry, I know I need to humble myself. I am certain that I need an understanding far greater than my own to trust. It would be utter foolishness not to get on my knees and ask God for his wisdom to guide me.

When we need to make an important decision and we are too proud to humble ourselves, we will assume we know best and refuse to consult others; or even if we know we need help, our fear of appearing foolish or weak will prevent us from asking others for the advice we need. Even worse, it is possible to be so proud that we do not feel the need to consult God for his input either.

Let me ask you a question. How has it worked out when you have run your life your way instead of God's way? Either you did not ask God for his direction or you knew God's will and chose yours over his.

Is there one time you can recall and say to yourself, "I am so glad I disobeyed God and chose my own path because it brought so much peace into my life and such great blessing into the lives of others"? Is there one time you can look back on and think, *If I had asked God for his direction and had done it his way, my life would be a wreck. But acting in my own wisdom instead of his was a great decision. Things could not have turned out more awesome?*

A question often attributed to Robert Frost contains great insight: How many things have to happen to you before something occurs to you? Let me add to his questioning: How many times do you have to make a mess out of your life before it occurs to you that God knows better than you? How many times do you have to bring pain to others' lives before it occurs to you that God's ways are better than your ways? How many times do you have to end up on your face, broken inside, alienated from people you love, and filled with shame before it occurs to you that you should humble yourself, quit leaning on your own understanding, ask God for guidance, and do things his way?

Humble yourself before God and before others. Admit your weakness and ask for his counsel and direction, and God will direct your steps.

There is a third prerequisite we are told is necessary to receive God's guidance: "in all your ways submit to him." How do we do this?

When the Bible Specifically Addresses Your Life Situation, Accept What It Teaches as God's Will

Paul tells us: "All Scripture is God-breathed and is useful for teaching, rebuking, correcting and training in righteousness" (2 Tim. 3:16). The Greek word translated as "God-breathed" in the New International Version is rendered as "inspired" in some other versions. But the meaning of the Greek word *theopneustos* (used only here in the New Testament) means more than our English word *inspire* often connotes. Sunsets inspire artists. Love inspires poets. The joys and sorrows of human existence inspire authors to write novels that try to explain the human condition. But Paul meant more in this verse than simply that contemplating the nature of God inspired the human authors of Scripture to pen deep and uplifting thoughts about how we should live. "God-breathed" means the words of Scripture originated with God, and through his servants he expressed his heart and his will. Consequently, the Scriptures are God's Word, authoritative for our lives, trustworthy in all they convey, and "useful for teaching, rebuking, correcting and training."

This means the Bible is God's instruction manual for our lives. Its purpose is to teach us God's will for our lives. Of course, it does more than that. It reveals the nature and character of a God who is so beyond our understanding that we could never comprehend him or his ways left to our own devices (Isa. 55:8–9). The Scriptures will cause us to marvel at the wonder of who God is and rejoice in the depth of his love for us. But they also have the very practical purpose of revealing God's will for our lives so we might be conformed to the image of Christ and walk in his ways.

The Bible does not speak to every specific situation we will face throughout our lives—which college to attend, which job to take, which person to marry. Nor is the Bible always easy to interpret. There are times when it is difficult to know exactly what it teaches on a particular topic. But when Scripture does address our situation specifically and clearly, what it teaches is God's will for us.

How does the Bible speak to our life situations? Often through direct commands that are very clear. "You shall not give false testimony against your neighbor" (Ex. 20:16). "You shall not commit adultery" (Ex. 20:14). "Honor one another above yourselves" (Rom. 12:10). "Do not repay anyone evil for evil" (Rom. 12:17).

The Bible will not tell us whom to marry. But it does tell us that believers are to marry believers (1 Cor. 7:39). The Scriptures do not tell us which job to take or what career to pursue. But it makes very clear the attitude we are to take to work and how to treat our colleagues. So even when God's Word does not give us specific instructions about a decision we need to make (whom to marry or which job to take), it still very often gives us direction and guidance about God's will for us in that situation.

In addition to the commands we find in Scripture, the Bible also reveals God's will for us another way—through the example of godly men and women, especially through the example of Jesus. He is "the Word . . . made flesh" (John 1:14 KJV), and as such, his life, as well as his words, reveal to us the mind and the will of God. Jesus loved and accepted people before he approved of their behavior. That's God's will for us. He cared deeply about the poor and the marginalized. That's God's will for us. He became infuriated in the face of injustice and false religion and he forgave those who hurt him. That's God's will for us.

How do we submit to God in all our ways? We ask ourselves, "What would Jesus do in this situation?" Asking and trying to answer that question may not tell us exactly what we should do, but it will often tell us what we should not do. That is God directing our steps and making our paths straight. That is his will for our lives.

If you want God to guide you, read and study his Word. Where it is clear, obey its commands and always seek to follow the example of Jesus that we find in the Bible. This is the primary way we submit to God in all our ways.

When the Bible Does Not Address Your Situation Directly, Make Wise Decisions

Just because the Bible does not tell you whom to marry, that does not imply that it does not matter whom you choose for a spouse. "Better to live in a desert than with a quarrelsome and nagging wife" (Prov. 21:19). And, of course, the converse is also true—better to live alone than with an angry and abusive husband. There's no surer way to be miserable than to marry the wrong kind of person. It's hard to do when we are young and fall in love, but even then the goal is to be wise when we are picking a spouse.

Some people choose their mates because it is a way of rebelling against their parents. That's not wise and, consequently, not God's will for you. Some people marry their spouses because they have lots of money. That's not wise and it's not God's will for you either. And it is certainly not a good idea to marry someone who is marrying you for your money. That is a surefire way of ending up miserable, alone, and broke.

So, if the Bible does not tell us exactly what to do in a particular situation—Should I marry this person? Should I go into business with this friend? Should I move to be closer to family? Is now the time to retire? How can I best help my child who is on drugs?—what is our guiding principle for acknowledging God and doing his will?

The apostle Paul wrote, "Be very careful, then, how you live—not as unwise but as wise, making the most of every opportunity" (Eph. 5:15–16). If your decision is not a moral issue and if the Bible does not address it specifically, we have a good deal of freedom in determining what course to take. But the goal is always to make wise decisions. How do we do that? Here are some guiding principles.

Put God first in your life

"The fear of the LORD is the beginning of wisdom" (Prov. 9:10). "Fear" in this verse does not mean we are to live afraid of God or in constant fear of making a wrong decision. It means living with the sense that we are accountable to God. He has given you a human life to use and invest however you choose. The life you have is so valuable in the sight of God that Jesus went to the cross to save it.

God has entrusted you with a human life. You can use it for an infinite number of purposes. Every day, with every choice, you determine what that purpose will be. Wisdom is knowing that at some time in the future you will return that life to God and there will be an accounting. You will say to him, "These are the decisions I made. This is what I did with the life you gave me. Here's how I treated it. Here's how I used it." Wisdom is living each day in such a way that when God reviews our life, he will respond, "Well done, good and faithful servant" (Matt. 25:23).

Wisdom begins when? Not when we know everything or even when we know more than most folks. The beginning of wisdom is recognizing that we are accountable to God for the life we live and the choices we make. Get that straight, and we are halfway home to making wise decisions.

Ask for wisdom

Humble yourself and ask for guidance, and you can trust what James wrote: "If any of you lacks wisdom, you should ask God, who gives generously to all without finding fault, and it will be given to you" (James 1:5).

God is the source of wisdom, and he will give us the wisdom we need if we will ask. His Spirit will speak to our spirits. Or he will bring the right people into our lives to help us. Or he will bring to remembrance past experiences that can teach us how to live in the present. But if we are open, if we humble ourselves and ask for understanding and insight, God will give us the wisdom we need to walk in his ways and do his will.

Seek wisdom from others

"Listen to advice and accept discipline, and at the end you will be counted among the wise" (Prov. 19:20). "Plans are established by seeking advice . . . Obtain guidance" (Prov. 20:18).

From whom should we seek advice? People who know God and who are spiritually mature. People who know us and will be both loving and honest. If possible, people who have been through what we are facing.

Often, though, we seek advice from people we believe will tell us what we want to hear.

A man is about done with his marriage. He is not happy with his wife, and he wants out. Who does he turn to for advice? The buddy who is divorced who will tell him what a wonderful decision he made by divorcing his wife. "Best thing I ever did was divorce my wife," his friend says. "I could not be happier. The children are doing fine. Life could not be better." Why does the man seek out this particular friend? Because he has heard his friend say these very things before and it is what he wants to hear so he can feel good about leaving his wife.

Either purposefully or subconsciously, this man does not go to a friend who went to counseling, thinking it would do no good, but who now has a happy marriage with the woman he was thinking about leaving. Why? Because he knows what he will hear: "It was hard work. I had to look at my own self and quit blaming my wife for my unhappiness. I had to crucify my ego and ask my wife for forgiveness, and I had to forgive her. Our marriage is not perfect, but it's good, and I am so grateful that God has kept us together."

Yes, go to people who have been through what you are facing. But do not go to those who will tell you what you want to hear. Find someone who will challenge you to think through your decision from all angles and, hopefully, from God's perspective. Their words may or may not be God's will for you, but often those who are a few steps removed from a situation can give us the perspective we cannot achieve when we are emotionally involved.

Have you ever been so ticked that you fired off a letter or an e-mail when you were still steaming? How did that work out for you? You felt very justified in telling the person how wrong he or she was and how deeply you were offended. I have done that, and usually, after some time has passed, I have regretted it. I have also sent that kind of e-mail to a third person and said, "Tell me what you think." Almost always the response has been, "I wouldn't send that, at least not the way you have it. How about this?" What that third person suggests is most times so much better than what I originally wrote.

Even when you feel very justified in your anger—no, especially when you feel justified in your anger—stop and seek out the wisdom of others before you act. Following their counsel may not be emotionally satisfying in the moment, but there is usually wisdom in their advice.

When we are not sure what to do, one of the ways we allow God to guide our steps is by talking to others about our problems. Seek out people who are mature in the faith and who have lived long enough to have learned from their own experiences and mistakes. That is the way of wisdom.

Consider a decision's impact on your previous commitments

"Lord, . . . who may live on your holy mountain? The one whose walk is blameless, . . . who keeps an oath even when it hurts, and does not change his mind" (Ps. 15:1–2, 4).

You have made commitments to God and to others. Some you have made explicitly, others implicitly. You have made promises to your spouse, your children, your church, your work, and your friends. Either with your words or by the very nature of your relationship with them, you have promised to be faithful to them, to seek their good, and to be there for them physically and emotionally as much as possible. Before you make a decision, make certain you will still be able to keep these prior commitments.

You are offered a great new job. The downside is you will have to travel so much you will barely be involved in the lives of your children as they are growing up. What was the commitment you made to them when you brought them into the world? You are their father or their mother. Was the oath you took, "I promise to be there when it's convenient, when it doesn't interfere with work or get in the way of my career?" Or did you promise that you would be fully invested and involved in their lives?

You want to purchase something but you have commitments to pay your bills, tithe to God's work, save for the future, and put money away for your kids' education. Taking on a new financial obligation that makes it impossible or difficult to keep those prior commitments is not God's will for you. Sure, it is disappointing not getting what you want because you have these other obligations, but sometimes that is what it takes to walk in the ways of God.

The church asks you to be in charge of an important ministry but you have young kids and already you feel that your wife is doing more than her share in raising them. The godly path may very well be saying no to the church and yes to your primary responsibility of being a caring husband and an invested father.

A man I know from the gym told me, "I have an invitation to go to the Super Bowl in San Francisco. A friend called me up and said he has a ticket for me and a place to stay, all free. I just need to get there."

"Man, that's incredible," I said. "Good for you."

He went on, "Yeah, I don't think I'm going."

"What are you talking about?" I asked incredulously. "How can you not go?"

With a gentle smile on his face, he said, "That weekend is my daughter's tenth birthday. That just seems more important to me."

Could he have done both, maybe celebrate his daughter's birthday a day early and still have gone to the game? I do not know the answer to that question. Maybe he could have and it would not have bothered her at all. But I do know this. We will never regret the time we spend with our kids or the sacrifices we make to be the loving, committed fathers or mothers they deserve and we promised to be when we brought them into this world. Something else I know: I could not have more respect for that man, and his daughter is blessed to have him as a father.

Keep your oaths and your obligations even when it hurts. It is not God's will for you take on other goals and responsibilities if they make it impossible to keep the important commitments you have already made.

Do something and trust that God will be at work

When you have sought the Scriptures and prayed, asked for the counsel of others, and considered your other commitments, and still you have several options that seem equally good—choose one and trust that God will guide you as you move forward. The way of wisdom is not to be paralyzed by indecision, never acting and afraid of making a mistake because you have not heard clearly from God. The way of wisdom is to trust in God's grace and in his sovereignty and to act as wisely as you know how.

God has promised that if we trust in him with all our hearts, do not lean on our own understanding, and submit our plans to him, he will make straight our paths. We do not trust that we will understand God's will perfectly. Or that we will always hear him right. Or that we will never make a mistake. We trust in the Lord with all our hearts that he will guide us. He will direct our steps and lead us into his will. We trust that God will redeem our mistakes, teach us through our errors, and direct our paths.

The Lord is our shepherd. He leads us in paths of righteousness for his name's sake. Therefore, we can walk through the darkest valley and fear no evil for he has promised to guide us even when our minds are uncertain and our hearts are frightened. And the promises of God are unfailing.

God, even as I struggle to know your will, this I am sure of: you are wise and you are good and you can be trusted. I confess that my understanding is lacking and my heart is often conflicted. I need greater wisdom than I possess within myself. So, I humble myself and look to you for direction. Show me in the Scriptures, bring the right people into my life, and open my heart to what is wise and good so I may walk in your ways. Even before I know what you desire, I commit, with your help, to be obedient. Speak, Lord, for your servant is listening. In Jesus' name, amen.

SIX

THE PROMISE OF POWER TO CHANGE

One reason I enjoy talking to nonbelievers is they make me think. They look at the world differently than I do, and they often challenge my beliefs. That kind of conversation is good for me, and it makes life interesting.

Several years ago I developed a friendship with one of the architects who was doing some work for the church I was serving. He was immensely talented and very bright. He believed some kind of higher power existed but nothing like the God who has revealed himself in Jesus.

Out of the blue one afternoon he asked me, "Do you think people really change?"

"Yes, of course," I said. "I wouldn't do what I do if I didn't think people could change."

He shook his head. "I don't. I think fairly early in life, we become who we are. Later in life, we may nibble around the edges a bit, but we don't change. Not really. Not much."

I told him of people I knew whose lives had been dramatically changed. What they wanted out of life, what they valued, how they spent their time and their money had been radically transformed. But even as I was talking, I thought to myself, *But not everybody changes. I wonder why.* I finished our conversation with these words: "Real change happens, but not as often as it should."

Of all the promises we will look at in this book, this one may be the most difficult to believe. You do not have to be who you have always been. You do not have to do what you have always done. You do not have to live the way you have always lived. You can be changed, and not merely in some kind of outward, cosmetic way so that your life may look different than it once did. The promise of God is that you can be changed from the inside out, and so much so that you are a new creation, a different person than you once were.

The promise that we can be transformed is the promise of the new covenant that was given to us through the coming of Christ.

> "The days are coming," declares the LORD, "when I will make
> a new covenant with the people of Israel and with the people
> of Judah. . . . This is the covenant I will make with the people
> of Israel after that time," declares the LORD. "I will put my law
> in their minds and write it on their hearts. I will be their God,
> and they will be my people." (Jer. 31:31, 33)

God promises in this passage that the new covenant will bring a new reality. Our hearts will be changed; his ways will be written into our very being. Following him will not be our trying to live up to the rules "out there" but living out the change he has made "in here."

The apostle Paul, on the other side of the cross, tells us that what God promised through Jeremiah has, in fact, happened in every person who has truly accepted Christ. "Therefore, if anyone is in Christ, the new creation has come: The old has gone, the new is here!" (2 Cor. 5:17).

Here's the same promise through the prophet Ezekiel: "I will give you a new heart and put a new spirit in you; I will remove from you your heart of stone and give you a heart of flesh" (Ezek. 36:26). The core affections of our hearts can be changed. The part of us that desires and yearns and loves, the part of us that decides what or whom we will seek after—our hearts can be changed and we can become new people.

Your Heart Needs to Be Changed

That may be hard for you to hear, but your heart needs to be changed. So does mine. Jesus said: "For it is from within, out of a person's heart, that evil thoughts come—sexual immorality, theft, murder, adultery, greed, malice, deceit, lewdness, envy, slander, arrogance and folly. All these evils come from inside and defile a person" (Mark 7:21–23).

I do not know who said it first, but it is the absolute truth: the heart of the human problem is the problem of the human heart. There is something wrong with us that originates at *the core of who we are*.

"Rob, are you telling me that I am a terrible sinner?" No, I do not think you are a terrible sinner. I think you are a terrific sinner. I think you are great at sinning. You are a natural when it comes to sinning. In fact, you are so adept at sinning that most of the time you do it without even thinking about it. Sadly, the same is true of me.

I am not telling you that you are a bad person or that you are as evil as you can be or that there is nothing good within you. But I do believe what Jesus taught. Our selfish acts and evil deeds come out of something that is wrong deep within us. That is where the problem resides and that is what needs to be changed.

"Trust your heart and you'll never be wrong." How many bad movies have you seen where that is the greatest insight and best advice that supposedly wise parents have to give their befuddled teenagers? "Just follow your heart, dear. Trust what it tells you, and you will always be right."

Really? I always want to ask the screenwriter: "Do you know so little about the human heart? Have you reached adulthood with no self-awareness or humility? Have you learned nothing from history or from your interactions with others? Do you honestly believe that our hearts are always right, always generous, always good?"

The human heart is proud. Yours is. So is mine. Your heart is self-serving. So is mine. Your heart is able to justify just about anything you desire if the payoff is big enough. So can mine. Your heart will hide its true motives from you and make you think you are fighting for some grand principle when it is doing nothing more noble than seeking greater power, higher position, more possessions, or some physical pleasure. That's what I've learned about my heart. And that's what the Bible teaches. "The heart is more deceitful than all else and is desperately sick. Who can understand it?" (Jer. 17:9 NASB).

If that is true—if it is even partially true that our hearts are deceitful and sick—the question is, How can we live a life that pleases

God? Yes, we can be forgiven for the past, but how can we live a new kind of life with the same old heart?

There is an ancient fable from India about a magician and a mouse. The mouse had done the magician a favor and the magician agreed to grant the mouse any wish he chose. The mouse had always been afraid of cats. For a long time he had thought, *If only I were a cat, I would never again be afraid.* So, he asked the magician to change him into a cat. The magician granted the wish.

Soon the mouse, now a cat, returned. He had encountered a dog and once again he was afraid. He asked the magician if he could be changed, this time into a dog as ferocious as the one he had seen. The magician once more worked his magic.

Later that day the mouse, now a dog, returned, trembling and anxious. He had seen a tiger, and fear had gripped his heart. He begged the magician to transform him once again. The magician thought for a moment and then acquiesced.

As night was falling, the tiger approached the magician. "Oh, great magician," he pleaded, "I have seen a lion and my heart is full of fear. Change me once more." The magician shook his head. "I have tried to change you, but I have failed. For though you have the body of a tiger, you still have the heart of a mouse."

Here's the trouble with too many good, religious folks who are trying to live the Christian life: they do not have the heart for it. You cannot live a new life with an old heart. You cannot live a different kind of life when you are the same old person.

One reason people reject the Christian faith is because they try to live like a Christian but it is frustrating and they fail. And either they become resentful toward a God who expects them to do what they cannot do or they become so discouraged and ashamed of themselves that they give up and walk away from the faith.

You and I have a problem. All people do. Our hearts are sick and sinful and selfish. If we are to live a new life, a life that pleases God, our hearts must be changed.

Your Heart Can Be Changed

The gospel promises we can not only be forgiven of our sins; we can also be set free from the power of sin. Here's the promise again:

> I will sprinkle clean water on you, and you will be clean; I will cleanse you from all your impurities and from all your idols. I will give you a new heart and put a new spirit in you; I will remove from you your heart of stone and give you a heart of flesh. And I will put my Spirit in you and move you to follow my decrees and be careful to keep my laws. (Ezek. 36:25–27)

The promise God gave his people through Ezekiel was twofold. He would "sprinkle clean water" on them and cleanse them from their impurities. This is a description of forgiveness and having our guilt removed in the sight of God. But there is more to the promise than being cleansed of our sin. God also promised he would give his people a new heart and put his own Spirit in them to move them to follow his commands. That is transformation from the inside out. That is the promise that we can be changed.

What follows are three approaches to the spiritual life. The first two are very common but absolutely deficient for a transformed life. They are little more than self-help projects, human beings trying to live a new life with an old heart. The third is God's way of changing us, making us into new people. As I describe these three approaches,

I will illustrate each one, using the testimony of a man I know well who was converted three years ago. I asked him to write his story for me, and I will quote from it extensively. Everyone's experience is not the same. Some of us have one huge moment of transformation. For others, it is more of a process. You do not have to have the same dramatic encounter with Christ that John did. But you do need to have your heart transformed by the Spirit of God.

Here's how John's story begins.

> For the first sixty-two years of my life, I did not know God. It would not be right to say that I hadn't found God because I wasn't looking. But God found me, and He has made all the difference in my life. For most of my life, I relied on myself above all. Then at age fifty-five, I found myself alone in a small apartment, divorced, isolated from my family, friends, and colleagues and sitting in a bathtub with a gun to my head. I remember being very calm about it. Let me tell you, there is no feeling as empty as when you realize the world has nothing for you.

John was raised in a home where there was no mention of faith. His father was an alcoholic and would walk around the house with a shotgun or a pistol, talking about killing everyone in the family, including himself.

John married a wonderful woman and became very successful professionally, working for a large oil company for thirty-eight years until he retired as an executive. Unfortunately, John learned to survive the dysfunction of his childhood by isolating himself emotionally. Of course, over time this led to problems in his marriage, until, finally, when she could no longer endure living with a husband who was distant, controlling, and judgmental, his wife divorced him. It was in the aftermath of his divorce that John found himself holding the same gun to his head that his father had carried around their home, threatening to kill him and the other members of his family when John was a boy.

We'll stop there with John's story for a moment and look at the first approach that many people take to living the Christian life.

The Information Approach

Information is "knowledge obtained from investigation or instruction."[1] People who adopt the information approach to spirituality assume, "The more I'm learning, the more I'm growing." They attend church, listen to sermons, read the Scriptures, and may even attend Bible study, not so much with the intention of forming a new life as with the purpose of informing an old mind.

After his divorce, John met a terrific woman who is a committed Christian and a member of our church. He began attending services with her. Without realizing what he was doing, he adopted the informational approach to changing his life. "I listened to the sermons and they resonated with me on a practical level, that is, good advice on how to live my life." He joined a Bible study and he enjoyed what he was learning. But that is as far as it went.

Unfortunately, this is as far as it goes for many people who attend church. For them sermons and Bible study are primarily about gathering information, learning more about God, and getting some good advice on how to live a better life.

This is a very Western approach to knowledge and to life. It is like a biochemist who thinks he knows all about romance because he can explain the electrical and chemical changes that occur in the brain when a person falls in love, but he has never fallen in love himself. It is like someone who has never had teenagers telling you how you should raise yours because she read a book on the subject. It is the man who can give you a definition of "faith" and point to the places in the Bible where people acted in faith, but all his life he has worked hard to keep himself from ever being in the place where he had nothing to depend on the promises of God.

In the West, we tend to believe we have mastered a subject when we can discuss it at length and describe it in detail. It never occurs to us that our relationship with spiritual truth is not about our mastering it, but about it changing and mastering us.

The informational approach to the spiritual life requires little personal experience with actual spiritual realities and no existential commitment to the truths we are learning. But it provides a person with the false comfort that he is on the right track because his knowledge is increasing.

People who employ this method of spirituality may or may not be growing more like Jesus. They may not over time become more compassionate or patient. They may not become more generous or more concerned about the poor. But they think they are growing because they now know the time line of the Old Testament, who wrote the book of Revelation, and the difference between justification and sanctification.

Information is important. The more we know, the more we can grow. But information alone is not enough. Knowledge by itself does not change the human heart or create a Christlike spirit within us. In fact, the tendency is the more we know, the prouder and less dependent on God we become (1 Cor. 8:1).

I am presently serving as a pastor at the Woodlands United Methodist Church for the second time. When I was appointed here right out of seminary, most of our members were in their late twenties to early forties. Many were just getting back into church as adults.

After six years, I left and served other churches for thirteen years and then returned to the Woodlands. Of course, the church had changed—more members, larger staff, expanded facilities, a wide variety of ministries for people of all ages. But what impressed me most was that some of the men I had worked with earlier had been transformed. What they thought about and talked about was different. What they valued, how they spent their time, what gave them joy—they were not the same men I had known thirteen years earlier. How they defined themselves and their purpose—Christ was right at the center of it all. They prayed like men who knew God, and they lived like men who wanted to please him. They had been transformed from well-meaning guys who knew a little bit about God into men who were spiritually mature and seeking first the kingdom of God. When I had left they were walking around in spiritual diapers, and now the kids were all grown up and doing well.

There was something that I found even more surprising—shocking, really. There were other men in the church I had known who were very similar to the men I just described. Same age, same community, same professions, same church for the past thirteen years. Sadly, the best I could tell, they were also the very same spiritually as when I had left. They had sat in the same pews and had heard the same sermons. They had been in the same Sunday school classes and had had all the same opportunities for growth. But from everything I could see, they thought the same way, wanted the same things, and were living the same life as they were thirteen years before.

Two groups of men. They had received the same information. Some of their lives were being changed into the image of Jesus, with new priorities, new commitments, and a new way of living. But the other men seemed to be no different than they were thirteen years earlier.

Does real change occur in the lives of people? Yes. But it does not happen as much as it should—almost never for men and women who take an informational approach to the spiritual life.

The Reformation Approach

To "reform" is "to put or change [something] into an improved form or condition."[2] It is the desire for reformation that causes many people to start attending church or reading the Bible. They want to improve themselves and change their lives in a positive way.

Maybe they have a problem with impatience or anger. Or they find themselves anxious and depressed, or they keep repeating the same self-defeating patterns and they want to change. It could be they have lost a relationship they once valued, and they are insightful enough to understand that they need to work on themselves rather than blaming the other person.

When people reach the point that they want to change their lives, they very often think, *I need to reform my ways and start doing things differently. Maybe the church can help me work on myself and become a better person.*

We can certainly appreciate the desire for self-improvement and if that gets people to church, so much the better. It was this desire that moved John to begin to look for some answers. "After the low point in my apartment, I knew I was going to have to live differently but I wasn't sure how to change." When we realize we need to change, the question that follows is, But how? Is there something I need to learn? Is there something I need to start or stop? Do I just need to focus and try harder at being a better person?

When a person comes to the conclusion that he needs to change, he has a very important question to answer: What is the cause of the dysfunction that has made a mess of my life and hurt others? It is a question we all must answer. Is my problem—my selfishness, my impatience, my anger, my lack of spiritual growth—is it in my life because I have not learned enough or tried hard enough? Or is there something wrong inside me that trying harder will never fix?

When people want to reform their lives, they usually turn to willpower. They think, *I will focus my attention on my problem. I will exert my will and work hard to change myself.*

But there is a problem. Your willpower does not determine what you desire. All it ever does is attempt to achieve what you desire. Willpower does not create the core affections of your heart. It only works to satisfy the core affections you already possess. What if there is something wrong with what you desire? What if there is something broken inside you—sick, even? What if your heart—the seat of your desires, the part of you that determines what you value and what you pursue—what if there is something wrong with that part of you? Then your willpower will never be enough to live a different kind of life.

You can fight your nature. For a time you may be able to contain it. You might be able to drive it underground for a while. But you will not be free of it until it is transformed.

Willpower says, "By the strength of my own will, I will change myself. I will tell myself to be different. I will hate the part of me that's ugly and mean and self-centered. I will tell it to go away and never return."

But as long as our hearts are wrong, our willpower will eventually express the wrong that is within them. As long as our hearts are angry or lustful or greedy or malicious or insecure, we will continue to struggle with immorality, dishonesty, pride, and a temper that does damage to the people we love.

Why? Because willpower only expresses what is in the heart. It is powerless to transform the heart and its desires.

Again, from John,

> Leading up to my conversion, my focus had continued to be on myself, making myself a better person through my own efforts. It felt good to work at that and I made progress, but I was still burdened by my past sins and my inability to get past the sins of others. I still had issues periodically with anxiety and anger. My self-talk was relentlessly negative, focused on conflict and the slights and aggressions of others, real or perceived. My stress level was high and constant.

Look at the word *reformation*. It begins with *reform*. Our efforts at reformation take the old stuff that is inside us and reform it, reshape it, move it around, and reorder it. We might be able to make some progress in becoming a better person. But *reform*ation does not change the stuff that is already inside of us, the stuff we are made of. And reformation does not change what is wrong within our hearts.

We live in an age where people are easily offended. If my telling you there is something wrong with you is offensive to you, instead of thinking *wrong*, think *broken*. There is something broken, twisted, sick at the core of who we are, you and me included. The moral mistakes we make and the selfish patterns we repeat are less about the weakness of our wills than they are about the brokenness and the sickness of our hearts. As long as our hearts are broken and sick, our lives will never be right, no matter how strong our willpower, because all our wills ever do is express what resides within our hearts.

Here's what I have come to conclude about myself. See if it applies to you. I can make myself a better person, but I cannot make myself like Jesus. I can change my priorities, but I cannot change my nature. I can fight the twisted desires within my heart, but in my own strength I cannot win the battle.

If that is where you are, then this next approach to the spiritual life is for you.

The Transformation Approach

To "transform" is "to change in character or condition." A synonym for this word is *transfigure*, which means "to change a thing into a different thing."[3] Transformation is the promise of the gospel. Our natures can be changed. Our desires can be changed. The core affections of our hearts can be transformed, and we can become more like the Savior we love. The promise is not that we can transform ourselves, but that God can transform us.

Back to John—and Jesus.

I participated in my first mission to Honduras. One day during the lunch period, I walked alone into the tiny church on a mountaintop that was our base. Hanging on the walls of the church were simple banners on which were written the various names of God. The local pastor came up to me with an interpreter. He put his hands on my shoulders, looked me in the eyes, and said "I know you feel God calling you, and you are resisting him." When I returned from the trip, I started a study of the Gospel of John called *Who Is Jesus?* One night about 3 a.m. when I couldn't sleep, I was reading in the Gospel of John when I saw Jesus clearly and intensely in my heart and mind. I saw Him on the cross, beaten and bloody, and I knew at that instant that Jesus had died for my sins, not just the sins of others. I fell to my knees weeping, repented of my sins, and accepted Jesus as my Lord and Savior. This same experience happened again about one month later. I joined the church shortly after that and at age sixty-two was baptized by immersion in August 2016 in front of my brothers and sisters in Christ. After I accepted Jesus, everything changed, and it changed overnight.

John is a new man. I know him well and he is a different person now that he has Jesus in his life. His purpose has changed from living for himself to living for God. His priorities have changed. The concerns that once consumed him have become unimportant. His relationships have changed, primarily because he has changed. He now lives to serve God and others, especially the poor, and his prayer life has changed.

One last quote.

Before I accepted Jesus, I relied on myself to find my way in the world of men. In reality, despite outward evidence of worldly success and being considered a good person, I was just stumbling from one crisis to another. My self-gratification came from solving each crisis even as I knew that I probably caused many of them. Make no mistake; my life is far from perfect. But there is no mistaking the changes that have been made in me.

Not everyone's coming to faith is as dramatic as John's. But every one of us needs our hearts to be changed and every one of us can be transformed by God from the inside out. If you have truly accepted Christ, the transformation has already begun. As I mentioned before, Paul wrote, "Therefore, if anyone is in Christ, the new creation has come: The old has gone, the new is here!" (2 Cor. 5:17). If you have received Christ, God's Spirit lives in you. You have been born again and you are a new creation.

But even people who have had a dramatic conversion similar to John's will still discover that the total transformation of our hearts is an ongoing process. Our principal desires and the direction of our lives may be changed in a moment, but God bringing to completion the good work he has begun in us (Phil. 1:6) will continue throughout our lives, and we have a part to play.

Look at this encouraging passage: "Therefore, my dear friends, as you have always obeyed—not only in my presence, but now much more in my absence—continue to work out your salvation with fear and trembling, for it is God who works in you to will and to act in order to fulfill his good purpose" (Phil. 2:12–13).

Just to be clear, notice that Paul did not write "work for your salvation." Salvation is not a prize for good behavior or a payment for services rendered. It is a gift we receive by faith based not on what we do for God but on what God has done for us through the life, death, and resurrection of Jesus.

But Paul does say we must "work out" our salvation. In other words, we must put our salvation into practice, make it real in how we live, and labor diligently until our outer lives conform to the inner change God's Spirit has created within our hearts.

The good news in this process, according to Paul, is that God is working in us "both to will and to act." Even after accepting Christ, the spiritual life is not reduced to the changes we can make through our own willpower. God is at work in us "to will and to act." He will give us his strength to do his will and to work out our salvation.

So God is at work in our lives, giving us new desires and his strength to act on those desires. But we are the ones who are to "work out" our salvation until our lives are transformed outwardly as well as inwardly. How does that work?

There will certainly be moments when we will need to exert our will to be faithful to God. When we face temptation, when we become discouraged, when we must pick up a cross to follow Christ faithfully—we often have to dig deep and use all our strength to do God's will.

But ultimately, even after accepting Christ, the battle is not won by our willpower. It is won by letting God go deeper in our lives. This is how we receive the strength we need to overcome life's trials and temptations and how the continued transformation of our lives is "worked out" in how we live. This is the thought Paul expressed so well when he wrote, "Whoever sows to please their flesh, from the flesh will reap destruction; whoever sows to please the Spirit, from the Spirit will reap eternal life" (Gal. 6:8). How do we sow to the Spirit? Answering that question in depth would require another book, but here is a (too) brief summary of what the Scriptures teach.

Spend Time in the Presence of God

There is a curious passage in Exodus. It describes Moses as he returns to the Israelite camp after being with God on Mount Sinai.

"When Aaron and all the Israelites saw Moses, his face was radiant, and they were afraid to come near him" (34:30). Moses spent time in the presence of God and he was changed. In fact, he reflected the very nature of God. Moses did not work to reflect the character of God. He did not will himself to radiate the glory of God. It happened naturally, even without knowing it was occurring. It happened whenever he met with God on Mount Sinai. Each time he would return, radiating with a beauty and a glory that was not his own. This will not sound particularly theological, but the more time Moses spent with God, the more God rubbed off on him and the more Moses was changed into God's image. The same will be true for us. The more time we spend in the presence of God, the more we will become like him.

We cannot transform ourselves, but we can put ourselves in a place where God can change us. And that place is in his presence. That's one of the ways that we "sow to the Spirit." We spend time in the presence of God, opening our lives to him. Worship, prayer, reading and meditating on the Scriptures, fasting, receiving Holy Communion—they all make a place in our lives for God to meet with us. Whenever we create those spaces, God will come and he will rub off on us and we will be changed.

Jesus spoke the same truth to his disciples: "Remain in me, as I also remain in you. No branch can bear fruit by itself; it must remain in the vine. Neither can you bear fruit unless you remain in me" (John 15:4). We cannot produce the fruit of the Spirit—love, joy, peace, patience, kindness, goodness, faithfulness, gentleness, self-control—in our own strength or by our own will. They are produced within us only by being connected to the life that is in Christ.

We cannot live "the Jesus life" without the life of Jesus living in us. So, put yourself in a place where the life of Jesus is able to flow into your heart and mind.

Spend Time with Others Who Are Being Transformed

Very few of us march to our own drum. We are influenced by the people we spend time with, especially our close friends. We know this to be true. That is why we pray for our grown children who are not following Christ, "Lord, please bring someone into my child's life who will be a good example, who will love her and show her a better way." That is the reason when a child gets into trouble, we often shake our heads and say, "He fell in with the wrong crowd." We know that people (ourselves included) take their cues from those around them about how to think, what to value, and how to live.

The author of Hebrews wrote, "Let us consider how we may spur one another on toward love and good deeds, not giving up meeting together, as some are in the habit of doing, but encouraging one another—and all the more as you see the Day approaching" (Heb. 10:24–25). We need others in our lives who are striving to follow Jesus. Their words and their example will spur us on and encourage us to be faithful in living a Christlike life of love and good deeds.

Other than spending time with God, there may not be a more important way of "sowing to the Spirit" than sharing our lives with others who are living for Jesus. If you want to live a truly great life, spend time with truly great people. Fill your life with people of character. Surround yourself with people who are devoted to their spouses and invested in their children. Find others who are committed to Christ, growing in the faith and living as servants. They will inspire you and influence you to "work out your salvation" and express the new nature God has placed within you.

Do the opposite—fill your life with people who live for themselves, who possess the world's values, who have no higher purpose than making money and being happy, and who care nothing for the poor—and their words and their example will influence you. You will be more likely to live like the world than to live like Jesus.

Of course, we care about people and share our lives with people who do not yet know Christ or live in a way that pleases God. One of the reasons Jesus scandalized the Pharisees and the teachers of the law is that he welcomed sinners, spent time with them, and ate with them. So, no, we do not withdraw from the world and its needs.

But your friendships matter. Your relationships matter. Who you give access to your heart matters. They will influence how you think, what you desire, and how you live. Be intentional about spending time with people who with their words and their actions will inspire you to become more like Jesus and live a life that pleases God.

Spend Time in Challenging Places

In other words, get in over your head doing God's work. You know the saying, "Keep doing what you've always done and you'll keep getting what you've always gotten." But it is worse than that. Keep doing what you have always done and you will keep being who you have always been.

You and I need to be uncomfortable. We need to get into situations that raise questions that do not allow for easy answers or a shallow spirituality. We need to have experiences where we do not know what to think or what to do. To be transformed into the image of Jesus, we must get out of a world that is isolated and safe and churchy. We must step into places that are so needy and so full of pain that we feel what we have never felt, ask what we have never asked, weep as we have never wept, pray as we have never prayed, and experience God as never before.

We can read about poverty and we can read about a God who loves the poor; but until we have been among the poor, we will never understand poverty and we will never understand God's heart for the least and the last. We can read about a Savior who healed the broken and loved the despised; but until we have listened to their stories and cared for them ourselves, we will never fully know the heart of Jesus or the power of what his love can do in a life. And we will never be fully transformed into the image of Christ.

The same experiences that keep us comfortable keep us from being transformed. A predictable world, where our ideas are safe and unchallenged, will not change us. Caring for people in ways that do not require faith and courage will never create a heart that is adventurous and strong. Doing what we have always done will never produce a life that is deep or a heart that is wise. It will only create a life that is complacent and a heart that is small.

God has promised that you can be transformed. From the inside out you can be changed. God is at work in you both to will and to act. Your part is not to change yourself but to put yourself in a place where God can do his transforming work in your life. Put yourself in his presence often and deeply. Spend time close to others who are being transformed, and open your heart to them. Step into places that are difficult and challenging and ask God to teach you and grow you. Do these things and you can be confident that "he who began a good work in you will carry it on to completion until the day of Christ Jesus" (Phil. 1:6).

———————

God of grace and God of power, I confess that I am helpless to change myself. I cannot transform my heart or make right what is wrong within the deep parts of who I am. But you have promised to make me new, and that is my desire. I yearn to be like Jesus, with new desires and holy affections. I long to have his heart and to live as he did, forgetting myself and serving you. By your grace I will sow to your Spirit and put myself where you can do your work in my life freely and unhindered. In Jesus' name, amen.

———————

SEVEN

THE PROMISE OF STRENGTH TO ENDURE

Our scars tell our stories. They are the mile markers of our existence, reminding us where we have been. Like chapter titles, they announce what has been written onto the pages of our lives. Even as they cover and hide our wounds, they reveal to all that we have suffered.

As with a block of marble, what has been taken from us has created the contours of our being. How we have handled the pain of being human in the past has determined who we are in the present. What we do with our suffering today will form who we are tomorrow.

People get hurt in the world we live in. At times, we suffer because of the cruelty of our enemies. On other occasions, we are betrayed by a loved one or forgotten by a friend. But however it comes, we all end up wounded. No one gets through this life without scars.

If you want to live well in a world where people are hurt and mistreated, suffer deeply and unfairly, wounded not just in their bodies but also in their souls, it is important to hold on to God's promise: "My grace is sufficient for you" (2 Cor. 12:9). Whatever you face—temptations, trials, opposition—God will give you his grace, and his grace will be sufficient for you to overcome.

Looking back on our scars, there are times we can laugh about them. We may even brag about them, shaking them off, "It was nothing, really." We might even take a strange pride in having been hurt more severely or wounded more deeply than others. But in the moment, whether the wound is physical, emotional, or spiritual, when we are broken and bleeding, there is no laughter or pride. We wonder, *How deep will the wound go? How long will I have to endure such pain? How broken will I become? How scarred will I remain when this is over?*

God has a promise for us when our way is dark and the suffering is great. When we do not understand what is happening to us and our lives are in chaos, the unfailing promise of a faithful God is this: *"Whatever you face and however you suffer, you can hold on because my grace will be sufficient for you."*

These are the words that God spoke to Paul when he pleaded for God to take away his thorn in the flesh. "My grace is sufficient for you, for my power is made perfect in weakness" (2 Cor. 12:9). It is a promise that Paul wrote on God's behalf to all of us. "No temptation has overtaken you except what is common to mankind. And God is faithful; he will not let you be tempted beyond what you can bear. But when you are tempted, he will also provide a way out so that you can endure it" (1 Cor. 10:13).

The Greek word (*peirasmós*) translated as "temptation" in 2 Corinthians 12 can also be translated as "testing." It is often associated with physical suffering or spiritual attack.[1] The promise God gives us is that when we suffer to the point that our faith is tested and we are tempted to be unfaithful, he will give us the grace we need to endure the pain and remain true.

He Will Give You the Strength You Need to Overcome

Paul wrote to the church in Corinth that throughout his ministry he suffered from what he referred to as "a thorn in the flesh." Paul did not describe for the Corinthians what the thorn was. Very possibly they were familiar with his condition and understood his reference perfectly. But two thousand years later we are a bit in the dark. Some scholars have thought Paul was referring to the constant opposition and persecution he suffered. Others believe it was bouts of malarial fever. Some have suggested that Paul suffered from epilepsy. We know from his letter to the Galatians that he had an eye condition that caused him suffering and embarrassment, and some have argued that was Paul's thorn.

The literal meaning of the Greek word for "thorn" (*skolops*) in 2 Corinthians 12:7 means "something pointed."[2] It is sometimes translated as "stake" and refers to a sharpened piece of wood that was employed as an instrument of torture or execution. Whether Paul was referring to his affliction as a "thorn" or as a "stake" is unclear. But what is certain is that it was painful enough that Paul referred to it as "a messenger from Satan" and it caused him such torment that he pleaded not once, but three times, that God would remove it from him.

Here's how he described his condition in his second letter to the Corinthians:

I was given a thorn in my flesh, a messenger of Satan, to torment me. Three times I pleaded with the Lord to take it away from me. But he said to me, "My grace is sufficient for you, for my power is made perfect in weakness." Therefore I will boast all the more gladly about my weaknesses, so that Christ's power may rest on me. That is why, for Christ's sake, I delight in weaknesses, in insults, in hardships, in persecutions, in difficulties. For when I am weak, then I am strong. (2 Cor. 12:7–10)

Maybe you have been there or maybe you are there now—that place where it feels as if there is a thorn in your flesh. A stake has been driven through your heart. Satan is attacking you. You are so tormented in body and spirit that you do not know if you can bear any more. God's promise to you is this: "My grace is sufficient for you, for my power will be made perfect in your weakness."

God's grace will be enough for you. Not merely enough for you to endure. But enough for you to overcome. Enough to go through times of suffering, hardships, and even persecution and come out stronger in faith, closer to God, and powerful in your witness for Christ.

Have you ever known anyone with ALS (amyotrophic lateral sclerosis), commonly referred to as Lou Gehrig's disease? I have known two people who suffered with it. It is a hideous disease. It takes everything from you except the mind within you, which is keenly aware of all that you have lost.

Joseph was the first person I knew with ALS. He had been a firefighter before he was diagnosed. He was afflicted when he was in his thirties, much earlier than most who suffer with ALS. He and his wife had two young children. Joseph was very aware that he would not live long. He knew that when he died, he would leave behind his wife and children.

When you are a young pastor, as I was then, you so want to say the right words, read the right passage, or pray the right prayer that will bring comfort and hope to those who are suffering. You feel a burden to be a source of strength and encouragement. "What can I say, what can I do, that will help these dear folks?" you ask yourself and God.

I remember meeting Joseph for the first time. It was at his home. The first thing I noticed was the odd angle of his body, seated in a wheelchair. There were straps around his body and a chair that held him in place so he would not fall out. But quickly, my attention was drawn to the warm, broad smile on his face. I did not know it then, but I would find him smiling every time I visited him in the future. Joseph was at peace. He exuded a calm, immense strength. At the same time that his body was twisted and his fingers curled, he was beautiful to behold.

Self-pity? Not Joseph. He spoke at length about how grateful he was for his many friends and all they were doing for him and his family. Self-absorbed? No, he asked about others and how he could pray for them. Weak? Yes, physically. But his faith was strong. He talked about the many blessings he had enjoyed in his life and how good God had been to him.

How was he able to be this way? I dare to tell you this only because Joseph told me. "God's grace is sufficient." I have seen it. "In our weakness God's power is made perfect." It is strong enough to hold on to us when we are losing our grip on everything the world has to offer. It is sufficient for us to overcome fear and bitterness and self-pity.

The other person I have known with ALS was older. Peggy had been a committed follower of Jesus all her life. She possessed a brilliant mind and a servant's heart. Throughout her ordeal with the disease, she remained kind-hearted and gracious to others. She never complained or asked, "Why me?"

There came a time when Peggy could no longer talk or even squeeze my hand. But her eyes were clear and alive. I saw it. When someone spoke about her Lord, or the Scriptures were read to her, or friends would gather around her bed and sing the hymns she loved, her eyes would widen and brighten, and her witness was unmistakable. God is good and his grace is sufficient.

Peggy asked that a passage be read at her funeral from the book of Habakkuk. In that book the prophet questions God. His people are suffering while the wicked prosper, and he complains that it is unjust for God to allow this to occur. Habakkuk demands an answer from God.

"How long, LORD, must I call for help, but you do not listen?" (Hab. 1:2). For a full chapter he pours out his complaint. How long must we endure this pain? Why must we suffer? Do you no longer love us? Then Habakkuk declares, "I will stand at my watch and station myself on the ramparts; I will look to see what he will say to me, and what answer I am to give to this complaint" (Hab. 2:1).

God speaks to Habakkuk and promises justice and salvation, but he does not promise that they will come soon. In the meantime he tells the prophet, "The righteous will live by his faith" (Hab. 2:4 NASB).

There are times when life makes no sense, the righteous suffer, and we are left with no easy answers that resolve our questions or ease our pain. God says, "In those times if you want to live, you must have faith."

What passage did Peggy ask me to read at her funeral? Not "How long, LORD, must I call for help, but you do not listen?" Not, "I will stand my watch and see what answer God gives to my complaint." No, the passage she gave us as her final witness is what I believe is the most moving statement of faith in all the Bible.

> Though the fig tree does not bud and there are no grapes on the vines, though the olive crop fails and the fields produce no food, though there are no sheep in the pen and no cattle in the stalls, yet I will rejoice in the LORD, I will be joyful in God my Savior.
>
> The Sovereign LORD is my strength; he makes my feet like the feet of a deer, he enables me to tread on the heights. (Hab. 3:17–19)

The promise of God is true. He will give us grace, and his grace will be sufficient. The grace he gives may not be an end to our suffering or the answer to our questions. But it will be the grace we need to endure our pain and our confusion and to live a life that overcomes.

God promised that his grace would be sufficient for Paul. But was it? During his ministry, three times Paul was beaten with rods, once he was stoned by an angry mob and left for dead, three times he was shipwrecked, he was put in prison so often we are not sure just how many times, and on five different occasions he was scourged with thirty-nine lashes. But no matter how great the trial or how immense the suffering, each time Paul got up, went forward, and proclaimed the good news of Jesus Christ.

No man did more to spread the Christian faith in the first century than Paul, and no man suffered more for doing so. Paul faced constant opposition and persecution. He was forsaken by friends and often felt weak and, at times, alone. Yet, he never gave up. He remained true to Jesus and he changed the world. What explains a life like that? Paul says it was grace, God's grace that is made perfect in our weakness. You can be certain that God will keep his promise and give you the strength to overcome whatever you must face. His grace will be sufficient for you. Trust that promise, build your life upon it, and walk in it. You will find strength and you will overcome.

God Will Give You the Grace to Grow in Character and Become Whole

The pain we endure will either crush our spirits or make us stronger. It will leave us broken or make us better. It depends on how we respond.

When we are mistreated and hurting, we are likely to have one of two reactions. One is to protect ourselves from further hurt by becoming hard inside. Turn off emotionally, stop caring or feeling for others, put up walls that guard our hearts from the pain that compassion and openness can bring into our lives. Retreat to a place so far removed from the world that we are untouchable, invulnerable, never to be hurt again. Only later do we discover that the walls we have put around ourselves have not created a fortress where we are safe but a casket where we die.

But suffering may have a very different effect upon us. The pain we experience may open our hearts to others. Our anguish and sorrow may cause us to empathize with others who suffer and move us to genuine concern and acts of compassion. Our pain can move us to seek God in new and deeper ways and result in a closer relationship with him, real spiritual growth, and wisdom.

Our scars may tell our stories. Our wounds may make us who we are. But it is what we do with our pain and our suffering that determines whether we become like Jesus. The promise of God is that he will give us sufficient grace that our pain can be redeemed, our suffering can bring growth, and our hearts can become open to the needs of others.

The Department of Human Services and the National Endowment for the Arts have partnered with Walter Reed National Military Medical Center to help wounded warriors recover through music. Battlefield medicine and trauma care have vastly improved in the last few decades, meaning that more soldiers come home alive, but with more devastating injuries than ever before.

Marine corporal Tim Donley returned from Afghanistan, the victim of a roadside bomb that took both of his legs and the use of his right arm. In an interview with CBS News' David Martin, Donley was open about the emotional wound he suffered with the loss of his arm in particular. "I can't salute. And I can't shake somebody's hand. You feel helpless and hopeless . . . and it stings."

Donley and a band of brothers (others who have suffered debilitating injuries from their service) are finding encouragement and healing through learning and performing music together. Their most well-known concert is one they performed with Pink Floyd's Roger Waters, titled "Stand up for Heroes" at Madison Square Garden.

Donley has become known for his rendition of Leonard Cohen's "Hallelujah." In the song are the lyrics, "It's not a cry you can hear at night. It's not somebody who has seen the light. It's a cold and it's a broken Hallelujah."[3]

In his interview with Martin, Donley described the question he had to answer if he was going to move forward in life. "The next thing you know, my whole life is coming down around my ears. Every dream, every hope I've ever had for the future is broken around me, and I don't know where to turn, and it was at that place that God said, 'Do you still trust me? Do you still believe that I have what's best for you?' And it was at that moment that I understood 'Hallelujah.'"

Proclaiming "Hallelujah" when you are suffering and see no way out. Trusting God when it feels as if everything has been taken from you. Holding on to the promise that God knows what is best for you when the worst has happened. Believing that God's grace is sufficient for you. Does it make a difference? Donley ended his interview with these words: "I may be more whole now than I've ever been in my life."[4]

There are some lessons we cannot learn and some growth we cannot experience until we have nothing to hold on to but God. There will be times when we are hurting and confused. We will go through seasons when life makes no sense and we cannot imagine how our situation will change or how life will ever be good again.

In those moments God says, "Trust me. My grace is sufficient for you." It is what we do in those moments of pain and fear that determines who we become. Will we simply be people who are scarred? Or will we be people who are stronger and more whole now than before we were wounded?

How do you become a person of strength? You face intense trials and you persevere. How do you become courageous? You find yourself frightened and confused and you move forward. How do you develop character? You come to a hard place in life where there is no reward for doing what is right and maybe even a price to pay, and you decide your soul is more important than the prizes the world can give or the punishments it can inflict. How do you become a person of faith? You walk in the ways of God when it seems that you have not heard from God in forever. And when the night is dark and there's no light to be seen, you still cry out a cold and broken "Hallelujah."

The only way to grow in character is to struggle and to suffer and to persevere. But God promises if what you want is growth, his grace will be sufficient and through your suffering you can become strong and whole.

His Grace Will Enable You to Care for Others with Authenticity and Power

A few years ago I asked one of the attorneys in our church, a partner in one of the large firms in Houston, "Is it true? What I heard, that y'all are paying lawyers—their first year out of law school—$120,000 per year, is that true?"

He laughed and said, "Yep, it's true. And coming right out of law school, all they know is enough to mess things up."

It kind of works that way with us preachers coming out of seminary. We can really mess things up if we are not careful. This is primarily true of pastors like me, who go straight from high school to college to seminary to a church. We come out of school with all kinds of answers, almost as if life is a multiple-choice exam.

No matter what the question is, we can tell you which box to check. You have questions; we have answers—the ones they told us in preacher school. We are only too happy to pass out solutions the way a Pez dispenser doses out bad-tasting mints. At the end of the day, we go home feeling pretty good about ourselves and a little amazed at all the wisdom we were able to bestow upon others.

But how can you give out answers when you don't understand the questions? When you have not had enough life experience to know how much people suffer? When you have not yet lost something or someone who is dear to you? When you do not know what it is like to try your best only to see everything go wrong? How can you bring comfort to those who suffer when you have never known real pain yourself?

What people need when they are struggling, more than they need someone with the answers, is someone who knows the questions, who has lived the questions, and who for a time had to live without an answer. What people need is someone who can say, "I've been there. I've been in the dark where you are. I've hurt the way you are hurting. Look at my scars, I've been wounded too. I have been at that place where the night is dark and the road is long. I know what it is like to have nothing to hold on to but the promises of God. And he met me there. He was faithful there. His grace was sufficient for me there. And what he did for me, he will do for you. Until he does, I will walk with you."

In the United Methodist Church, we have bishops who appoint pastors to their congregations, usually with the advice of a district superintendent, who works closely with the pastors and churches under his or her care. One district superintendent told me about a young preacher who had all the gifts and possessed all the charisma any church could ever want. The bishop said to him, "I think that young preacher might be good for this church in your district."

But the district superintendent told the bishop, "I don't think so. At least, not yet. I don't want to be responsible for him."

The bishop asked, "Why in the world not?"

The superintendent answered, "Because he has never been broken. He has never failed."

That way of thinking may not make sense to people who are in business. But it makes sense to me. When it comes to caring for people who suffer and fail, we pastors do our best work not by giving out the best information, but by doing our best to understand, and to empathize with and to love flawed and hurting human beings. No seminary course, no professor, no textbook enables us to care for people who struggle as much as being broken and encountering the grace of God in the midst of our own devastation. Remembering our brokenness and the feelings of helplessness and hopelessness we experienced keeps us from offering easy answers that sound spiritual but are nothing more than trite platitudes that do nothing to bring strength and healing. Remembering God's grace in the midst of our brokenness allows us to speak words to others about God's faithfulness that are authentic and that can bring real hope to people who are hurting.

What is true of preachers is also true of you. You will help people more with your failures than with your successes, if you let God's grace go to your failures. You will help people more with your weaknesses than with your strengths, if you have learned to trust God where you are weak. You will help people more with the lessons you learned by falling on your face than with the times you walked on water, if you have let God pick you up, forgive your sins, and grow your character.

It may be human nature to believe what we have to offer is primarily our knowledge and our expertise. We think we will make a difference in others' lives based on our strengths and our successes. But I can assure you that what most profoundly impacts the lives of others is what we have learned through the grace of God meeting us in our struggles and failures.

If I help people who are hurting—if I help them find healing and if I help them grow through their pain—I believe there are two reasons. One is I try to be true to God's Word. The other is I try to be real about my own mistakes and failures and about how God's grace has helped me. I try to remember when I preach and teach that I am not giving a sermon or teaching a lesson; I am speaking to real people who have genuine questions, deep pain, and life situations that are overwhelming. When I do my job right and help people, it is because I remember the times I have struggled, been hurt, and failed, and those experiences inform everything I say and how I say it.

Being honest with ourselves and with others is essential. Not giving easy answers or even the right answers without first trying to understand the pain and the struggle behind the questions others are asking is imperative. That is what people need from me and from you. To be able to do that, we must ourselves experience the sufficient grace of God forgiving us when we have sinned, picking us up when we have fallen, healing us when we are wounded, and giving us a second chance when we do not deserve it.

It is then that we have a gift to give. It is then that we have a story to tell that will bring hope and strength to others. It is then that we can speak with authenticity and with the spiritual authority that comes not from knowing the answers, but from having lived the questions: Can God be trusted? Is his grace sufficient? Can he bring wholeness out of brokenness and failure?

Do not be ashamed of your scars or embarrassed by your wounds, whether they were self-inflicted or were brought on you by others. Your scars make you real. They give you a gift to share. They give you a story to tell that others will listen to and be helped by. It is your scars, not your perfection, that make you beautiful to those who need to know that God's grace will be sufficient for them.

Gracious God, I am broken, wounded, and scarred. But I am not ashamed. You love me as I am, and I will stand before you and the world honestly, unafraid to tell my story or to be seen for who I am. I will trust that your grace is sufficient to make me whole and to use me in the lives of others. And even when the night is dark and I cannot yet see the light, I will cry out, "Hallelujah!" In Jesus' name, amen.

EIGHT

THE PROMISE OF UNCHANGING LOVE

When I was a high school student, through the influence of a summer youth director, I came to have a personal relationship with Jesus. I had grown up in the church, was a good kid, went to youth group, and read the Bible every night.

For about a year before that summer began, I had started to wonder how I could know I was going to heaven when I died. I knew some people were going to heaven. I had read that in the Bible. But I wondered what percentage would make the cut.

I knew I was not perfect, but I was about to go to college, and I had heard the most wonderful news. In college they graded on the curve. So if the test was extremely difficult and if no one did really well, you did not have to make a 90 to get an A. You just had to beat out most of the other students.

When it came to pleasing God, I knew nobody was going to be perfect. Again, I had read my Bible and knew that everyone sinned. So, no one was going to make a perfect score on God's test. But some people were going to heaven. So, obviously, God was going to have to grade on the curve.

I began to ask myself, *What percentage will make it?* The Bible, the best I could tell, did not give us the answer. But I figured the top 10 percent for sure would get in. Probably if you were in the top 20 percent, you would be okay.

I looked at the other kids I knew. The competition, as I thought of them. Many of them were drinking. Some were using drugs. Most of the guys I knew used foul language. And some were having sex, maybe not as many as said they were; but still many were, or getting as close as they could. And those were just the other kids in our church youth group. I figured the kids not going to church were even worse.

I did not do any of those things. I went to church, I read the Bible, and I prayed. I put 10 percent of the money I made at my summer job into the offering plate on Sunday. "Hmm. I've got to be in the top 20 percent," I told myself. "Probably in the top 10 percent. I should be fine. If good people get into heaven, I will probably be okay." (Of course, at this point I did not realize that spiritual pride, of which I was guilty, is the sin that God despises most.) My fear of missing out on heaven was abated, and I became pretty comfortable with the idea that when it came to eternity, I was good to go.

Before I finish the story, let me stop and say that some of the people who will read this book, maybe you, are where I was. You may be a bit more sophisticated in your thinking than I was as a teenager, but it is possible that you believe good people go to heaven and you are a good person. You are a good husband or wife. You are a caring parent. Sure, you have some faults, but compared to others, when it comes to morality and integrity, you fare pretty well. You should be okay when you stand before God.

If the life you have lived is what you are depending on to be accepted by God; if your goodness is what you are trusting to make you right in his eyes; if your confidence for eternity is that you are as good as most and much better than many, then you need to hear very clearly that you are guilty of the worst kind of pride and you are in the gravest kind of peril. If you do not come to understand spiritual reality better than you do now, every verse of the Bible is clear that you will be lost when the day of judgment comes. To believe that you can stand before a holy God and be accepted because you are clothed in a righteousness of your own making means that you do not understand the holiness of God or the sinfulness of your heart, or both.

What helped me? I saw in my youth director, Eddie Wills, someone who had a relationship with Jesus. What I saw in him was so beautiful that I wanted it for myself. I saw Eddie had a relationship with God; I had a religion about God. He had a heart that was humble; I had a spirit that was proud. He had something real; I had an illusion I had created. He had a Savior; I had a hope that God would grade on the curve.

The only thing I can say to my credit is that when I saw what was real and true and beautiful, by God's grace, I wanted it for myself and I accepted Christ.

Within the next year I felt a desire to go into the ministry. I wasn't certain that God was calling me, but I was certain there were many decent people in my denomination, the United Methodist Church, who were trusting in their own goodness for their salvation. I remember telling God, "I don't know exactly what preachers do.

And once I find out, I may not be able to do it very well. But I can tell people about Jesus and how to accept him and how they can have a relationship with you. So unless I hear you telling me not to, that's what I'm going to do."

That is what I have done for thirty-six years as a pastor, and that is what I am doing in this chapter. I am sharing with you God's great promise that you can be saved. You can be forgiven, you can know God, you can experience an abundant life in this world, and you can enjoy eternal life with God in the world to come.

The promise that we can be saved is given to us in many places and in many ways throughout Scripture. But the most familiar is: "For God so loved the world that he gave his one and only Son, that whoever believes in him shall not perish but have eternal life. For God did not send his Son into the world to condemn the world, but to save the world through him" (John 3:16–17).

I once had a good Methodist member of the church I was pastoring say to me very sincerely, "We don't believe in all that salvation stuff, do we? That's what the Baptists believe, right?"

I told him, "Well, that salvation stuff is all throughout the Bible, including the verse that more people love and have memorized more than any other."

"All that salvation stuff" is at the heart of the way Jesus described his mission. He said of himself, "The Son of Man came to seek and to save the lost" (Luke 19:10). "All that salvation stuff" is why Jesus believed he had come to earth.

In fact, even his name is about all that salvation stuff. When the angel appeared to Joseph to tell him that his fiancée, Mary, had conceived a child by the Holy Spirit, he said, "She will give birth to a son, and you are to give him the name Jesus, because he will save his people from their sins" (Matt. 1:21). Jesus (*Yeshua* in Hebrew) means "the Lord saves." Why was he to be given that name? The angel said, "because he will save his people from their sins."

Jesus came into the world because we needed saving from our sins. That is why he came to planet Earth. That is how he defined his mission. That is what his name proclaims.

Where do we begin with this promise? With this: *God loves you, and you matter more to him than you know.* That's where John 3:16 begins: "For God so loved the world."

I had what I would describe as a "God moment" when my boys were very young. It is the most amazing thing when the nurse places your newborn child in your arms for the first time. I remember feeling love like I had never felt before. I loved my wife. I loved my parents. I loved my brother and sister. I loved my friends.

But the love I felt for my son when I held him the first time was different from anything I had ever experienced. It was instantaneous. It had nothing to do with what he had done for me or might one day do. It was just there, overwhelming, deep, and strong. And without any expectations. All the love was flowing from me to him for no other reason than he was mine. My child. My son.

A few years passed and his brother came along. There it was again, the same feelings of affection and concern and the desire to protect and provide all that I could for him.

Ten years went by, and we had a great day together. And I thought to myself, *Isn't it amazing how much I love my sons, how much they mean to me, how much joy they bring me just by being with me?*

Then I had the strangest thought. I wondered, *Is it possible that my parents love me this way? Is there any way that I could mean as much to my father as Stephen and Ian mean to me? Is it possible that being with me brings him the same kind of joy that being with my sons brings me?* Immediately I answered my own question: *Of course, not.*

That's crazy. There's no way he could feel about me the way I feel about my sons.

But then I thought, *What makes you think that as a father, you are something special? Why does what you feel for your children have to be any greater than or different from what other parents feel for their children? Or what your father and mother feel for you?* My immediate reaction was, *If that's true, if that is even the slightest bit true, I need to be better about calling my parents and going to see them.*

But I was not done. I heard myself ask another question: *Is it possible that God feels that way about me? Could it be that my heavenly Father loves me like that? Is there any way that he finds joy when I spend time with him and open my heart to him? Could I possibly matter to God the way my sons matter to me?*

I know it sounds crazy. Just the thought that God loves you that much, cares about you that deeply, yearns to have you that close, finds that much joy in being with you. That is crazy, right? Right. It is the crazy, unfathomable, vulnerable love that God has for you. You matter to God.

God could have chosen to relate to you as his employee. He could have set up a relationship with you where you work for him, he appreciates your labor, and he blesses you according to your efforts. That would be a great privilege. He could have decided to relate to you as his friend. If he called you a friend and left it at that—he cared about you the way you care about your best friends—that would be mind-blowing amazing. But the relationship God desires to have with you goes much further. He wants to love you and relate to you the way a father loves his child.

Look how Jesus described the God he came to reveal. "Which of you, if your son asks for bread, will give him a stone? Or if he asks for a fish, will give him a snake? If you, then, though you are evil, know how to give good gifts to your children, how much more will your Father in heaven give good gifts to those who ask him!" (Matt. 7:9–11).

In this passage Jesus tells us that as messed up as we are—as selfish as we are, with all of the mixed motives we possess, and with all of our impure thoughts—still we love our children and want to provide them with all they need. How much more, Jesus says, does your heavenly Father, who is nothing but goodness, desire to provide for you? How much more do you matter to him and how much more does he desire to bless you with his love and his good gifts?

This is the starting place of the promise we are given in John 3:16. God loves you more than any earthly father has ever loved his child. You matter to him. He wants you in his life. He wants you to share your heart with him. He wants to bless you with all that is truly good, including his loving presence in your life.

That is where the promise starts, but it is not where the promise ends. The promise that you can be saved has within it the message that you must be saved. In other words, *your need is desperate.*

If our lives matter to God, then it matters to God what we do with our lives. If you matter, your choices matter. If you matter, then what you give your heart to, what you put into your mind, and what you do with your body matters. If you turn the spirit within you into something that is self-centered and proud, bitter and brutal, angry, greedy, or lustful—it matters immensely. If your life matters, then it matters what you do with the life you've been given. And if God is the one who has given you the life you possess, when you fail to choose his ways, you do not sin simply against yourself or others; you sin against him.

The Bible leaves no doubt that in God's sight, we have all sinned: "For all have sinned and fallen short" (Rom. 3:23). "We all, like sheep, have gone astray, each of us has turned to our own way" (Isa. 53:6).

"If we claim to be without sin, we deceive ourselves and the truth is not in us (1 John 1:8).

We are sinners. All of us. You are. I am. Quoting Psalm 14, Paul summed it up this way: "There is no one who are righteous, not even one" (Rom. 3:10).

Some of us go through life with few regrets, not experiencing much guilt, feeling pretty good about ourselves. I said it before: psychopaths never feel guilty. Narcissists rarely do. People whose highest goal in life is being happy can usually justify their actions and escape the accusations of a healthy conscience.

But not feeling guilt does not mean it is not there. If you can look at your life and feel no remorse, it is not because you have lived a perfect or even a righteous life. It is because you are so far removed from the light of truth that you cannot see the reality of your sins for what they are. If you believe that one day you will stand before a holy God and in the light of his purity be untroubled by the ugliness of your heart and the sinfulness of your life, you have no understanding of God's holiness or the depth of your sin.

Couldn't God simply choose to ignore our sins and decide to act as if our misdeeds do not truly matter? Only if he is willing to act as if we do not matter. God could choose not to care about your sins, but only if he chose not to care about you—your life, your being whole, your being righteous. But you do matter to God, the way my sons matter to me, so he cannot act as if what you do with your life does not matter to him.

Richard John Neuhaus wrote,

We could not bear to live in a world where wrong is taken lightly and where right and wrong finally make no difference. Spare me a gospel of easy love that makes of my life a thing without consequence. . . . Atonement is not an accountant's trick. It is not a kindly overlooking; it is not a "not counting" of what must count if anything in heaven or on earth is to matter. God could not simply decide not to count without declaring that we do not count.[1]

So, God must care about our sins. But how much does he care? Do we get a slap on the wrist for our sins? Does he put us in time-out? Do we have to go to our rooms and think about what we've done?

If only sin were such a small thing. If only God were more like us and cared as little about transgressions as we do. But God is holy, absolute goodness, and purity. Sin not only mars the beauty of his creation; it offends his very being. He cannot act as if sin does not matter unless he is willing to deny his very nature.

So the Bible tells us, "The wages of sin is death" (Rom. 6:23). God takes sin so seriously that it separates us from him, and it will be judged in the severest of ways.

Back to the promise of John 3.16: "For God so loved the world that he gave his one and only Son." What a nice, sweet-sounding phrase, "*he gave his one and only Son.*" But it was not nice. It was not sweet. It was horrendous. Jesus was spat upon. His back was torn apart with thirty-nine lashes. Spikes were driven through his wrists and his ankles. Jesus was stripped naked as men mocked him and called him a fool. Then Jesus, hanging a cross, blood weeping out of his body, and his spirit in anguish cried, "My God, my God, why have you forsaken me?" (Matt. 27:46). The Father watched his Son being tortured and crucified, hearing the Son he loved cry out his name but having to turn away. *That* is what the Bible means when it says God gave us his Son for the sins of the world.

Do you want to know how much it matters that we have sinned? Then look at the cross. That's how much sin matters to God. That's how much being able to forgive you matters to him.

Do you understand how offensive it is to think, *I have lived a good life. I am better than most folks. When I stand before God, I will tell him that he should accept me because I have tried to live a decent and moral life*? Do you grasp what arrogance it is to think you can justify yourself, excuse yourself, save yourself, when the Father thought that the only way to pay for your sins was the death of his Son? If there was any other way, the Father would have chosen it. But there was not. The One who was righteous had to die for the unrighteous. The One who was sinless had to make atonement for the sinful. The One who owed nothing had to pay with his life the debt of those who owed a debt they could never pay. The One who is Jesus had to die for the one who is you.

The wages of sin is death. Either that penalty will be paid by you with your death, eternally separated from God, or it will be paid by Jesus on the cross. But one way or the other, your sin will be judged.

It has been said that "desperate times require desperate measures." You tell me: if the measure required for your salvation was the death of Jesus, how desperate must your condition be without him?

The promise of salvation found in John 3:16 says that *you must first accept what God has done for you.* You must "believe in him."

Christianity is not a code of ethics that tells us how to be moral. It is not a philosophy to explain our place in the universe. Christianity is not a religion that gives us objective facts about God. It may do all those things, but it is more than that.

Christianity is not a self-help program for prideful people who still have not come to grips with the fact that they cannot solve their biggest problem or save themselves by their own efforts. The

Christian faith is good news about what God, out of his love, has done for us in Jesus Christ. And it is an invitation to receive the gift of forgiveness and redemption bought for us by his death on the cross. Like every gift, it must be received.

John tells us, "He came to that which was his own, but his own did not receive him. Yet to all who did receive him, to those who believed in his name, he gave the right to become children of God—children born not of natural descent, nor of human decision or a husband's will, but born of God" (John 1:11–13).

How do sinful people like us enter into a right relationship with God? How do we become his children and experience the love of our heavenly Father? John says we must "receive" Jesus, by believing in his name, which you will remember means "the Lord saves." In other words, we must give up the idea that we can save ourselves, and we must trust not what we do for God, but what he has done for us.

Let me contrast two ways of becoming right with God and being saved. One way is our way. It is the way of fallen men and women, the way of pride and ego. The other is the way of God. It is the way of the gospel and the way of humility and grace.

HOW WE BECOME RIGHT WITH GOD

According to human nature
- By our merit
- Based on our goodness
- Based on our virtuous works for God
- By something we earn
- Through religion

According to the gospel
- By God's mercy
- Based on God's grace
- Based on Christ's work on the cross for us
- By something we're given
- Through relationship

The gospel of Jesus Christ is different from our egos and from the other religions of the world because when it comes to being made right with God, the gospel does not say "do." It says "done." The gospel does not say, "Achieve it"; the gospel says, "Receive it."

You must choose one of these two ways of becoming right with God. One appeals to our pride and says we can do enough to meet God's standards and save ourselves. The other is utterly devastating to our egos and says we cannot do enough. And there are some who cannot humble themselves and accept it.

In the movie *Get Low*, Robert Duvall plays Felix Bush, a 1930s Tennessee hermit who intends to throw his own funeral party while he is still alive. As a young man, Felix had had an affair with a married woman. When the woman's husband learned what she had done, he became enraged and killed her. Felix blamed himself, and for the next forty years, deprived himself of any form of happiness.

In a moving scene, he thinks of the greatest joys that men experience and he says he has had none of them—no wife, no children, no grandchildren. He says to a friend with great sadness, "I wouldn't even know how to hold a baby"—all of this in an attempt to atone for his sin.

If it sounds sad to you, it is. But there is more to it than that. In another scene, Bush tries to arrange his funeral with the local preacher, Reverend Horton. Here's their conversation.

Rev. Horton: What matters when you come to the end of
    your life is that you're ready for the next one. Have you
    made peace with God, sir?
Bush: I paid.

Rev. Horton: Well . . . you can't buy forgiveness, Mr. Bush. It's
free, but you do have to ask for it.

Bush: Nothing in this world is free, preacher.[2]

With that, Bush walks out of the church. What is behind his words,
"I paid"? "Nothing in this world is free." It is pride. It is the pride that
says, "I will pay for my own sins; in fact, I already have. If I have to ask
for forgiveness, then I'll go without. I have done enough that I am not
beholden to anyone. Not even to God."

It may not be that dramatic with us. But it is that same spirit that
causes people to say, "I have done enough, been good enough, lived
well enough, paid enough. I should be fine."

That is the world's way of getting right with God and being saved.
But it is not God's way. Salvation is not something we achieve; it is
something we receive. It is not a reward we earn; it is a gift we accept.

For many people it is offensive to be told there is no way they can
make themselves right with God. It is so different from how they live
the rest of their lives. Give them a challenge and they meet it. Give
them a goal and they reach it. Give them a problem and they solve it.

Then the gospel comes along and tells them that the problem
they are facing in the most important area of their life is something
they cannot fix and their only option is to humble themselves and ask
for grace. That is an offensive message. It always has been. "God was
pleased through the foolishness of what was preached to save those
who believe. Jews demand signs and Greeks look for wisdom, but we
preach Christ crucified: a stumbling block to Jews and foolishness to
Gentiles" (1 Cor. 1:21–23).

Two thousand years ago, the message that we are saved by
believing in a crucified Savior, not by our good deeds or our wisdom,

was offensive to the proud. It still is. But you can either hold on to your pride or you can have Jesus. You can cling to the idea that somehow you will save yourself, or you can humble yourself and accept Jesus as your Savior. But you cannot do both.

What must we do to receive this gift? John says we must believe in Jesus. "For God so loved the world that he gave his only-begotten Son that whoever believes in him . . ." (John 3:16). Belief (or "faith," which is translated from the same word in the Greek) in the New Testament, is more than mental assent to a propositional truth. Believing in or putting our faith in Jesus means we trust his claims completely, we place our lives into his care, and we live fully committed to him and his call upon our lives. Believing in Jesus means trusting him as the atoning sacrifice for our sins and dedicating our lives to him as our Lord.

The promise of salvation is a promise that *you will live in relationship with God forever.* The promise is "whoever believes in him shall not perish but have eternal life" (John 3:16).

The Greek word for "eternal" (*aiwnios*) is difficult to translate. It does contain the meaning of "everlasting, unending." But it is more than that. It also describes a kind of life we can know while we are still alive on earth. John 3:36 tells us, "Whoever believes in the Son has eternal life." The verb in that sentence is in the present tense—"has." Eternal life is a kind of life we can experience in the here and now through faith in Jesus.

John describes the most important characteristic of the new life we are offered this way: "Now this is eternal life: that they know you, the only true God, and Jesus Christ, whom you have sent" (John 17:3). Eternal life is the kind of life we experience when we are in relationship with God, when we are personally connected to him, and we know his presence in a real and personal way. This is how we were meant to live, in fellowship with God. Knowing God is the reason we were created, and it is the reason why the things of this world are never enough to satisfy the deepest longings of our souls. When we put faith in Jesus, we receive this new kind of life. We come alive inside with a life that is so full and so real that it will never end.

That is what I saw in my summer youth director when I was a teenager, wondering how I could be certain I would go to heaven when I died. I did not know what it was when I first saw it, but it was the life that God gives a person who has accepted Christ. Eddie knew the one true God and Jesus Christ, whom he sent. He had a personal relationship with God. He had a different kind of life than I did, and it was beautiful.

I told you earlier in this chapter that shortly after accepting Christ, I felt called to tell people how they could know Jesus as their Savior. Good people, going to church, needed to know that their goodness would not save them but the God who loved them would. That was my calling.

It could be that you are the reason I was called. God wanted you to hear the message of his grace and he knew that one day you would read this book and his Spirit would speak to your heart. If so, what should you do?

Say a simple prayer. Admit that you have sinned. Confess your desperate need for grace and mercy. Give up any illusion that you can save yourself. Ask God in his grace to forgive your sins. Trust in Jesus as your Savior. Invite him to come into your life and to teach you how to follow him.

If you do this, there is a promise for you: God loves you. God loves you so much that he gave his only Son to die on the cross for you so you might not perish but share life with him forever. It's a promise you can trust. If you will only receive it, you will discover that it is a promise that can save you.

———————————

Heavenly Father, I dare to believe that I matter to you, that you love me, and that you want a relationship with me. Thank you for giving your Son Jesus so I might be forgiven and saved from my sins. I acknowledge my sin and confess I cannot save myself. Without your grace I would be lost. But I now ask for your grace and I trust in Jesus and the death he died for me. I accept him as my Savior. Please give me the grace to follow you from this moment on, all the days of my life, and I will be yours. In Jesus' name, amen.

———————————

NOTES

Chapter One: God's Promises to You

1. Jessica LaGrone, Rob Renfroe, Andy Nixon, and Ed Robb, *Under Wraps: The Gift We Never Expected* (Nashville, TN: Abingdon Press, 2014). Adapted from *Under Wraps*. Used by permission.

Chapter Two: The Promise of Forgiveness

1. Werner Foerster, "Diaballoo, Diabolos," in *Theological Dictionary of the New Testament*, vol. 2, eds. Gerhard Kittel and Geoffrey Bromiley, trans. Geoffrey W. Bromley (Grand Rapids: Eerdmans, 1964), 71.
2. L. L. Morris, "Satan," in *The New Bible Dictionary*, ed. J. D. Douglas (Grand Rapids: Eerdmans, 1973), 1145–47.
3. Mary Poplin, "As a New Age Enthusiast, I Fancied Myself a Free Spirit and a Good Person," *Christianity Today*, December 21, 2017.
4. Rudolpf Bultmann "Aphiēmi," in *Theological Dictionary of the New Testament*, vol. 1, eds. Gerhard Kittel and Geoffrey W. Bromiley, trans. Geoffrey W. Bromiley (Grand Rapids: Eerdmans, 1964), 509–12.

5. Claudia Eller, "COMPANY TOWN: Top Dollar for Movie Idea," *Los Angeles Times*, October 14, 1994.

6. David Plotz, "Joe Eszterhas: How Did a B-Movie Screenwriter Become an A-List Celebrity?" *Slate,* March 15, 1998, http://www.slate.com/articles/news_and_politics/assessment/1998/03/joe_eszterhas.html.

7. Charles Lawrence, "A Battle of Basic Instincts," *Telegraph*, February 13, 2004, https://www.telegraph.co.uk/culture/film/3612158/A-battle-of-basic-instincts.html.

8. Joe Eszterhas, *Crossbearer: A Memoir of Faith* (New York: St. Martin's Press, 2008).

9. Joe Eszterhas, "My Base Instincts and God's Love," OnFaith, September 9, 2008, https://www.onfaith.co/onfaith/2008/09/09/my-base-instincts-and-gods-lov/6021.

Chapter Three: The Promise of New Purpose

1. Augustine, *The Confessions of Saint Augustine*, ed. F. J. Sheed (London: Sheed and Ward, 1984), 1.

2. Blaise Pascal, *The Thoughts, Letters and Opuscules of Blaise Pascal*, ed. and trans. O. W. Wight (New York: Derby and Jackson, 1859), 247.

3. Phyllis Thompson, *Sadhu Sundar Singh: A Biography of the Remarkable Indian Disciple of Jesus Christ* (Singapore: Genesis Books, 2007), 28.

4. David Bloom, quoted in Eric Metaxas, "But Sweet Will Be the Flower: The Life and Death of NBC's David Bloom," Eric Metaxas's official website, http://ericmetaxas.com/writing/essays/david-bloom-1963-2003/.

5. "Morton Kondracke: The Dick Staub Interview," *Christianity Today*, August 1, 2002. https://www.christianitytoday.com/ct/2002/augustweb-only/8-12-21.0.html.

6. Clayton Christensen's website, accessed September 28, 2018, http://www.claytonchristensen.com/.

7. Clayton M. Christensen, "How Will You Measure Your Life?" *Harvard Business Review*, July–August 2010, https://hbr .org/2010/07/how-will-you-measure-your-life.

Chapter Four: The Promise of Constant Presence

1. Nola Taylor Redd, "How Big Is the Universe?" Space.com, June 6, 2017, https://www.space.com/24073-how-big-is-the-universe.html.
2. Elizabeth Howell, "How Many Galaxies Are There?" Space.com, March 19, 2018, https://www.space.com/25303-how-many-galaxies -are-in-the-universe.html; Maria Temming, SkyandTelescope. com, July 15, 2014, "How Many Stars Are There in the Universe?" https://www.skyandtelescope.com/astronomy-resources/how-many -stars-are-there/.
3. G. K. Chesterton, *The Complete Father Brown Stories*, ed. Michael D. Hurley (London: Penguin Classics, 2012), 681.
4. Johannes Schneider, "Homoios," in *Theological Dictionary of the New Testament*, vol. 5, eds. Gerhard Kittel and Geoffrey Bromiley, trans. Geoffrey W. Bromiley (Grand Rapids: Eerdmans, 1964), 197.
5. Edward Shillito, *Jesus of the Scars: and Other Poems* (London: Hodder and Stoughton, 1919), vii, 73. (I am quoting three of four verses.)
6. Quoted in Jon Krakauer, *Where Men Win Glory: The Odyssey of Pat Tillman* (New York: Anchor Books, 2010), 197–98.
7. Edgar A. Guest, *You Can't Live Your Own Life* (Chicago: Reilly and Lee, 1928), 76–77.

Chapter Six: The Promise of Power to Change

1. Merriam-Webster.com, s.v. "information," accessed September 28, 2018, https://www.merriam-webster.com/dictionary/information.
2. Merriam-Webster.com, s.v. "reform," accessed September 28, 2018, https://www.merriam-webster.com/dictionary/reform.
3. Merriam-Webster.com, s.v. "transform," accessed September 28, 2018, https://www.merriam-webster.com/dictionary/transforming.

Chapter Seven: The Promise of Strength to Endure

1. Heinrich Seesemann, *"Péira,"* in *Theological Dictionary of the New Testament*, vol. 6, eds. Gerhard Kittel and Geoffrey W. Bromiley, trans. Geoffrey W. Bromiley (Grand Rapids: Eerdmans, 1964), 28–32.

2. Gerhard Delling, *"Skolops,"* in *Theological Dictionary of the New Testament*, vol. 7, eds. Gerhard Friedrich and Geoffrey W. Bromiley, trans. Geoffrey W. Bromiley (Grand Rapids: Eerdmans, 1971), 409–13.

3. Leonard Cohen, "Hallelujah," on *Various Positions*, Columbia, 1984.

4. "Band of Brothers," *CBS News Sunday Morning*, Interviewer David Martin, November 10, 2013.

Chapter Eight: The Promise of Unchanging Love

1. Richard John Neuhaus, *Death on a Friday Afternoon: Meditations on the Last Words of Jesus from the Cross* (New York: Basic Books, 2000), 9.

2. *Get Low*, directed by Aaron Schneider, performed by Robert Duvall and Gerald McRaney, Sony Pictures Classics, 2009.